ESSAYS

ESSAYS

WALLACE SHAWN

Haymarket Books
Chicago, Illinois

First published by Haymarket Books in 2009
© 2009 Wallace Shawn

Haymarket Books
P.O. Box 180165, Chicago, IL 60618
773-583-7884
info@haymarketbooks.org
www.haymarketbooks.org

Trade distribution:
In the U.S. through Consortium Book Sales and Distribution, www.cbsd.com
In the UK, Turnaround Publisher Services, www.turnaround-psl.com
In Australia, Palgrave Macmillan, www.palgravemacmillan.com.au
All other countries, Publishers Group Worldwide, www.pgw.com/home/worldwide.aspx

Special discounts are available for bulk purchases by organizations and institutions. Please contact
Haymarket Books for more information at 773-583-7884 or info@haymarketbooks.org.

This book was published with the generous support of the Wallace Global Fund.

Library of Congress Cataloging-in-Publication Data is available
ISBN 978-1-60846-002-1

Printed in Canada
2 4 6 8 10 9 7 5 3 1

CONTENTS

to Jonathan Schell and Deborah Eisenberg

in meditation (J.S.) and in fiction (D.E.): reality, truth, accepting it all; but then—intense, passionate dreams about extraordinary cities, a world where people live in harmony

1951—talks on the state of the world begin with J.S. after eighth birthday party

1972—meet D.E.—shocked by her views— discussion of China leads to tears

INTRODUCTION

The human community is carved up into "individuals." Why? Presumably because it's helped us to survive, because a sleeping dog can easily be kicked, but it's hard to damage a large group of flies. I honestly don't know. At any rate, I didn't ask to be an individual, but I find I am one, and by definition I occupy a space that no other individual occupies, or in other words, for what it's worth, I have my own point of view. I'm not proud to be me, I'm not excited to be me, but I find that I *am* me, and like most other individuals, I send out little signals, I tell everyone else how everything looks from where I am. I have more free time than a lot of individuals, so, instead of talking, I sometimes write. My friends Anthony and Brenda found my signals interesting, so Anthony asked me to collect them into a book.

I've always somewhat hated being "me" and only me. I wrote my first play at the age of ten, fifty-five years ago, and I've always found it a fantastic relief to imagine I know what things would be like from the point of view of other individuals and to send out signals from where I actually am *not*. Playwrights never need to write from the place where they are. Unlike the fiction writer who says, as himself, "Fred woke up in his bed that cloudy Sunday," a playwright can spend a lifetime writing without ever speaking from his own location.

I've passed my life largely in a fantasy world. My personal life is lived as "me," but my professional life is lived as other people. In other words, when I go to the office, I lie down, dream, and become "someone else." That's my job.

I've worked in the theatre since 1970. I've written plays and a few screenplays, in each one of which a person who isn't me speaks, and then another person who isn't me replies, and then a third one enters or the first one speaks again, and so it goes until the end of the piece. I've even worked as a professional actor, speaking out loud as if I were someone not myself. And perhaps it's disturbing or frightening how easy it is to become "someone else," to say the words of "someone else." It really doesn't feel odd at all, I have to tell you.

Every once in a while, though, I like to take a break from fantasyland, and I go off to the place called Reality for a brief vacation. It's happened a dozen or so times in the course of my life. I've looked at the world from my own point of view, and I've written these essays. I've written essays about reality, the world, and I've even written a few essays about the dream-world of "art" in which I normally dwell. In a bold mood I've brooded once or twice on the question, Where do the dreams go, and what do they do, in the world of the real?

My congenital inability to take the concept of the inviolable "self" seriously—my lack of certainty about who I am, where I am, and what my "characteristics" are—has led me to a certain skepticism, a certain detachment, when people in my vicinity are reviling the evil and alien Other, because I feel that very easily I could become that Other, and so could the reviler. And this has had an effect on my view of the world.

I grew up listening to discussions about the world, and in school I studied history and politics and even a little elementary economics. My parents were completely (some might say excessively) assimilated American Jews whose own parents (said with only a moderate degree of certainty to have been born in Sweden, England, Germany, and possibly Canada) were probably all of Eastern European or Russian origin, or in other words, saved from a harsh destiny by the existence of the United States of America. My mother and father, fortunate members of the bourgeoisie, were American liberals of the old school. They never described the United States as "the greatest country in the world" as many politicians did. They were passionately close to their French friends and their English friends and presided over a living room in which people from India, Poland, Italy, and Czechoslovakia were constant visitors, and they adored and admired Adlai Stevenson. From an early age, I remember going with my mother to the gorgeous, modern United Nations buildings on our own island of Manhattan and buying holiday cards from UNICEF in the United Nations gift shop.

(As a Jewish atheist, my mother was one of the world's most loyal devotees of Christmas, and she loved Advent calendars, Christmas trees, and Christmas cards.) Mother loved UNICEF, the United Nations Children's Emergency Fund, which helped poor children all over the world, and she loved the United Nations; and, to her, being an American meant being a person who loved the United Nations and was a friend to poor children all over the world, like Eleanor Roosevelt and Adlai Stevenson.

When not totally preoccupied with my own problems, I feel some of the emotions my mother felt toward those poor children all over the world. But my earliest essay, "Morality," from 1985 (I was just over forty years old when I wrote it) shows me slowly seeing, as it appeared out of the mist, the outline of my own figure as a character in their story. It turned out that my role was sinister, dreadful, but for my first forty years I hadn't realized that. My ignorance about my own involvement in the story of the children allowed me to think, Yes, the conditions in the world are terrible, certainly—but I still could feel that the topic could be discussed in a leisurely manner. When one hasn't noticed that it's one's own boot that's standing on the suffering person's neck, one can be calmly sympathetic to the suffering person and hope that over time things will work out well for them.

I never became as nice as my mother. But by the time I was forty-five I understood a few things that she'd overlooked. I suppose I'm something like what my mother would have been if she'd gone down into her basement and stumbled on Eleanor Roosevelt murdering babies there.

The schizophrenic nature of this book (essays on war and death and essays on the windowless miniature world of theatre) gives a pretty good picture of my own mind. Born by most definitions into the ruling class, I was destined to live a comfortable life. And to spend one's life as a so-called "creative artist" is probably the most comfortable, cozy, and privileged life that a human being can live on this earth—the most "bourgeois" life, if one uses that phrase to describe a life that is so comfortable that no one living it would want to give it up. To lie in bed and watch words bump together until they become sentences is a form of hedonism, whether the words and sentences glorify society and the status quo or denounce them. It's very agreeable to live like that, even if people don't like your work, criticize you, whatever. So I've always been tempted to turn off the radio and forget the world, but I'm not quite enough of a hedonist to forget it entirely and forever. I'm unable to totally forget the world—but I still haven't (yet) become a compassionate enough person to leave my bed for more than a moment in order to devote myself to *changing* the world or alleviating the suffering of my fellow human beings.

In other words, I've been divided, like this book. When I was fifteen, my brain was feverish with the work of Dostoevsky and James Joyce. But by the time I was twenty I'd turned against art, I planned to spend my life as a civil servant, helping humanity, and I would no more have dreamed that I'd one day work in the theatre than that I'd one day become a champion racing car driver. Five years later I'd fallen hard for art again, and I was loyal to art for twenty years. Then its immorality became intolerable to me, and I turned against it again, though I failed to find, as I looked around me, anything else that I wanted to do. At any rate, the oscillations continued, their pattern unpredictable and indecipherable to me.

Not surprisingly, my own ambivalence leaves me totally in awe of those amazing people whose concerns and passions have stayed constant and undimmed throughout their lives. I find I do need models or heroes to guide me on my journey through the world, and this need, combined with my shaky grasp on who I find "myself" to be, led me not merely to seek out and interview the poet Mark Strand and the political philosopher Noam Chomsky, but to believe, against the evidence, that they *were me*, and so I insisted that these interviews were essays of mine and had to be included as part of this book. Of course one could say that no one person could *be* both Noam Chomsky and Mark Strand, not merely because it's miraculous that anyone ever was remarkable enough to be *either* of them, but because their lives seem to point in opposite directions. That doesn't seem to stop me from wanting to be both of them at the same time, and it doesn't seem to stop me from refusing to accept that their lives are contradictory. Somehow poetry and the search for a more just order on earth are not contradictory, and rational thought and dreams are not contradictory, and there may be something necessary, as well as ridiculous, in the odd activity of racing back and forth on the bridge between reality and the world of dreams.

April 2009
New York City

PART ONE

REALITY

ONE

THE QUEST FOR SUPERIORITY

2008

When I was five years old, I had a small room of my own, with a record-player and records and shelves full of books. I listened to music, I thought up different kinds of stories, and I played with paper and crayons and paint.

Now I've grown up, and thank God things have mostly gone on as before—the paper, the stories—it's pretty much the same. I've been allowed to become a professional maker of art, I've become a writer, and I dwell in the mansion of arts and letters.

When I was a child, I didn't know that the pieces of paper I used had been made by anybody. I certainly didn't know that almost everything I touched had been made by people who were poor, people who worked in factories or on farms or places like that. In fact I'd never met anyone who worked in a factory or on a farm. I'd frequently met people who *owned* factories and farms, because they lived all around us in the huge houses I could see from my window, although I wasn't aware then that the houses *were* huge because the people who lived in them paid very low salaries to their employees,

19

while paying themselves enormous sums. Our wealthy neighbors were really like the giants in a fantastic tale, giants who were superior to others because they could spin gold out of human suffering.

Well, it turns out that I still live in the same neighborhood, because that's where the mansion of arts and letters is located. So I still can see giants when I look out my window, and the funny thing is that pretty much all of us in the mansion of arts and letters actually live off the money we get from these giants. Isn't that funny? You know, they buy the tickets to our shows, they buy our books and paintings, they support the universities where we teach, there are gifts and grants—it all comes out of the gold they've spun. And we live with them, we share the streets with them, and we're all protected by the same cops.

But you see, some of the people who *don't* live in the neighborhood—the ones our neighbors don't pay well, or treat well?—some of those people are out of control, they're so miserable, so desperate, they're out of their minds, they're very *threatening*, so it turns out we need more than cops. We actually have a large army as well, and a navy and an air force, plus the F.B.I., Coast Guard, Central Intelligence Agency, and marines—oy. It turned out that simply in order to be secure and protect our neighborhood, we needed an empire.

Some of us who live in the mansion of arts and letters are a bit touchy about our relationship to our wealthy neighbors. Bob, for example—he's a painter who lives down the hall from me—he refuses to bow to them when they pass him in the street, but, you know—they buy his paintings just the same. For me, though, it's my relationship with the poor people *outside* the neighborhood that I sometimes brood about in the middle of the night. It's the fact that so many of them are in agony that's in a way thought-provoking.

One evening last week, a friend and I went to a somewhat inexpensive restaurant, and the waiter who served us was in such a state of agitation or anxiety about God knows what that he didn't even look at us. And so I was thinking about the fact that in more expensive restaurants, the staff is usually trained to focus their attention on the pleasure of the diners, not on their own problems. In fact, the waiters in more expensive restaurants are invited to be friendly, amusing, to make funny remarks about their lives, to let us diners get to know them a little. But in the *most* expensive restaurants, the really fancy ones, we don't get to know the waiters at all. The waiters in those restaurants don't make funny remarks. They do their work with such discretion that they're barely noticed. And people compliment them by saying that they're unobtrusive.

Actually that's quite a good word for all those people whom we don't know and don't think about much but who serve us and make the things we need and whose lives we actually dominate: "the unobtrusives." And the interesting thing I've noticed is that in those very expensive restaurants, we don't talk with the waiters, but we enjoy their presence enormously. We certainly wouldn't want them to be replaced by robots or by conveyer belts that would carry our food to us while we sat in the dining room completely alone. No, we want them there, these silent waiters, these—"unobtrusives."

It's obviously a characteristic of human beings that we like to feel superior to others. But our problem is that we're *not* superior. We like the sensation of being served by others and feeling superior to them, but if we're forced to get to know the people who serve us, we quickly see that they're in fact just like us. And then we become uncomfortable—uncomfortable and *scared*, because if *we* can see that we're just the same, well, *they* might too, and if they did, they might become terribly, terribly angry, because why should they be serving us? So that's why we prefer not to talk to waiters.

A king feels the very same way, I'd have to imagine. He doesn't really want to get to know his subjects, but he nonetheless enjoys the fact that he has them. He finds it enjoyable to be told, "Your Majesty, you have ten thousand subjects." And in fact he finds it even more enjoyable to be told, "Your Majesty, you have a million subjects," even though he may never see them. The subjects are in the background of his life. They're in the background of his life, and yet they provide the meaning of his life. Without his subjects, he wouldn't be king.

Some people like to feel superior because once they were made to feel inferior. Others, including myself, were told constantly in their early days that they *were* superior and now find themselves to be hopelessly addicted. So, if I get into a conversation, for example, with a person who knows nothing about me, I immediately start to experience a sort of horrible tension, as if my head were being squashed, because the person I'm talking to is unaware of my superiority. Well, I have at my disposal an arsenal of indicators of superiority that I can potentially deploy—I can casually allude to certain schools I attended, to my artistic work, to the elegant street on which I grew up—but if, by analogy to some of those Tantric exercises one reads about, I attempt to follow the counterintuitive path of not revealing any of these clues—well, it's simply interesting to observe that I can rarely manage to hold out for as long as ten minutes before forcing my interlocutor to learn the truth about me.

Weirdly, it turns out to be possible for a person to feel superior because someone somehow *connected* to them has been raised up above others—a friend, an acquaintance, a parent, a child—and the connection can be even vaguer than that. I have to admit, I take a certain pride in Gustav Mahler's symphonies—after all, he was Jewish, and so am I. And Emily Dickinson was born in the United States, just like me. Incidentally, one unmistakable way to know you're superior to someone is to beat them up. And just as I feel rather distinguished if a writer from the United States wins the Nobel Prize, I also feel stronger and more important because my country's army happens to dominate the world. The king doesn't need to meet his subjects in order to enjoy his dominion over them, and I don't need to go to Iraq to know that there are people all over the world, a great number of quiet "unobtrusives," who experience a feeling of stomach-turning terror when they see soldiers wearing the uniform of my country approaching their door in the middle of the night. Now, let's admit that some of the rougher people who seem to thrive in our country, people like George Bush or Dick Cheney, for example, may perhaps take actual pleasure from the thought of our country's soldiers smashing in the door of some modest house in some godforsaken region of the planet, forcing a family to huddle on the floor, administering kicks in the face to anyone they like. Perhaps there may even be a modest clerk in a bank in Kansas or a quiet housewife on a farm in Idaho who feels a bit of enjoyment at a thought like that. But what bothers me more is that although I have nothing but contempt for imperial adventures, I've marched in the streets to demonstrate for peace, and I don't make it a practice to wink or joke about the brutal actions of brutal men, I can't deny that in spite of myself I derive some sense of superiority from being a citizen of a country that can act brutally with impunity and can't be stopped. I feel quite different from the way I know I would feel if I were a citizen of Grenada, Mauritius, or the Tongan Islands.

My feeling of superiority, and the sense of well-being that comes from that, increases with the number of poor people on the planet whose lives are dominated by me or my proxies and whom I nonetheless can completely ignore. I like to be reminded of these poor people, the unobtrusives, and then I like to be reminded of my lack of interest in them. For example, while I eat my breakfast each morning, I absolutely love to read my morning newspaper, because in the first few pages the newspaper tells me how my country treated all the unobtrusives on the day before—deaths, beatings, torture, what have you—and then, as I keep turning the pages, the newspaper reminds me how unimportant the unobtrusives are to me, and it tries to tempt me in its articles on shirts to consider different shirts that I might want to wear, and then it goes on, as I turn the pages, to try to coax me into sampling different forms of cooking, and then to experience different plays or films, different types of vacations…

It's become second nature to me to use the quiet crushing of the unobtrusives as a sort of almost inaudible background music to my daily life. Like those people who grow bizarrely nervous if they don't have a recording of something or other quietly playing on their sound system at dinnertime, we've become dependent over the course of decades on hearing the faint murmur of cries and groans as we eat, shop, and live.

How will the world change? Believe me, those who are now unobtrusive have their own ideas about how the situation might improve. But in the middle of the night I wonder: Can we in the mansion of arts and letters play a part? Could we reduce the destructiveness of the people we know? Could we possibly use the dreams we create to lure our friends in another direction? Because it's valuable to remember that the feeling of superiority is not the only source of human satisfaction. Imperial dreams are not the only dreams. I've known people, for example, who've derived satisfaction from collecting seashells. And sometimes I think of a woman I knew a long time ago who seemed to be terribly happy, although her life consisted of not much more than getting up each day, playing with the cat, reading a mystery, eating an agreeable sandwich for lunch, then taking a walk in the afternoon. No wealthy giant eating dishes costing hundreds of dollars could ever have enjoyed a meal more than this woman seemed to enjoy her simple sandwiches—so what was her secret? And what about Edgar, who gets such pleasure out of working as a nurse, or Tom, who finds such nourishment teaching children in school? Jane's need for superiority seems fully satisfied if a friend admires one of her drawings. And Edna's overjoyed if she wins at cards. People can make a life, it seems, out of love—out of gardening, out of sex, friendship, the company of animals, the search for enlightenment, the enjoyment of beauty. Wait—isn't that our particular province?

Beauty can be important in a person's life. And people beguiled by the beautiful are less dangerous to others than those obsessed by the thought of supremacy. If an afternoon of reading poetry has given me a feeling of profound well-being, I don't then need to go out into the street and seek satisfaction by strangling prostitutes. Art can be central in a person's life. If the art we create is beautiful enough, will people be so drawn to looking at it that they'll leave behind their quest for power? Beauty really is more enjoyable than power. A poem really is more enjoyable than an empire, because a poem doesn't hate you. The defense of privilege, the center of our lives for such a long time, is grim, exhausting. We're exhausted from holding on to things, exhausted from trying not to see those unobtrusive people we're kicking away, whose suffering is actually unbearable to us.

In the mansion of arts and letters, we live like children, running and playing up and down the hallways all day and all night. We fill room after room with the things we make. After our deaths, we'll leave behind our poems, drawings, and songs, made for our own pleasure, and we won't know if they'll be allowed to help in the making of a better world.

TWO

AFTER THE DESTRUCTION OF
THE WORLD TRADE CENTER

NOVEMBER 2001

To: The Foreign Policy Therapist
From: The United States of America
November 12, 2001

Dear Foreign Policy Therapist,

I don't know what to do. I want to be safe. I want safety. But I have a terrible problem: It all began several weeks ago when I lost several thousand loved ones to a horrible terrorist crime. I feel an overwhelming need to apprehend and punish those who committed this unbearably cruel act, but they designed their crime in such a diabolical fashion that I cannot do so, because they arranged to be killed themselves while committing the crime, and they are now all dead. I feel in my heart that none of these men, however, could possibly have planned this crime themselves and that another man, who is living in a cave in Afghanistan, must surely have done so. At any rate I know that some people he knows knew some of the people

29

who committed the crime and possibly gave them some money. I feel an overwhelming need to kill this man in the cave, but the location of the cave is unknown to me, and so it's impossible to find him. He's been allowed to stay in the cave, however, by the fanatical rulers of the country where the cave is, Afghanistan, so I feel an overwhelming need to kill those rulers. As they've moved from place to place, though, I haven't found them, but I've succeeded in finding and killing many young soldiers who guarded them and shepherds who lived near them. Nonetheless, I do not feel any of the expected "closure," and in fact I'm becoming increasingly depressed and am obsessed with nameless fears. Can you help me?

To: The United States of America
From: The Foreign Policy Therapist

Dear United States,

In psychological circles, we call your problem "denial." You cannot face your real problem, so you deny that it exists and create instead a different problem that you try to solve. Meanwhile, the real problem, denied and ignored, becomes more and more serious. In your case, your real problem is simply the way that millions and millions of people around the world feel about you.

Who are these people? They share the world with you—one single world, which works as a unified mechanism. These people are the ones for whom the mechanism's current way of working—call it the status quo—offers a life of anguish and servitude. They're well aware that this status quo, which for them is a prison, is for you (or for the privileged among you), on the contrary, so close to a paradise that you will never allow their lives to change. These millions of people are in many cases uneducated—to you they seem unsophisticated—and yet they still somehow know that you have played an enormous role in keeping this status quo in place. And so they know you as the enemy. They feel they have to fight you. Some of them hate you. And some will gladly die in order to hurt you—in order to stop you.

They know where the fruits of the planet, the oil and the spices, are going. And when your actions cause grief in some new corner of the world, they know about it. And when you kill people who are poor and desperate, no matter what explanation you give for what you've done, their anger against you grows. You can't kill all these millions of people, but almost any one of them, in some way, some place, or to some degree, can cause damage to you.

But here's a strange fact about these people whom you consider unsophisticated: Most of the situations in the world in which they perceive "injustice" are actually ones in which you yourself would see injustice if you yourself weren't so deeply involved in creating the situations. Even though they may dress differently and live differently, their standards of justice seem oddly similar to yours.

Your problem, ultimately, can only be solved over decades, through a radical readjustment of the way you think and behave. If the denial persists, you are sure to continue killing more poor and desperate people, causing the hatred against you to grow, until at a certain point there will be no hope for you. But it's not too late. Yes, there are some among your current enemies who can no longer be reached by reason. Yes, there are some who are crazy. But most are not. Most people are not insane. If you do change, it is inevitable that over time people will know that you have changed, and their feelings about you will also change, and the safety you seek will become a possibility.

THREE

"MORALITY"

1985

When I was around thirteen, I was sitting on a sofa with an older woman, and she said to me rather fiercely, "You don't understand this now, but when you get older, you'll come to appreciate the importance of comfort." This did turn out to be true. At that time, I really didn't have much to be comforted about or comforted from, so naturally comfort didn't matter to me then. And now it does. And the older I get, the more I long to feel really comfortable. But I've also come to realize that an awful lot of preparatory work must be undertaken before that particular feeling can begin to exist, and I've learned, too, how all that effort can count for nothing if even one tiny element of the world around me refuses to fit into its necessary place. Yes, I'm at home in my lovely apartment, I'm sitting in my cozy rocking chair, there are flowers on the table, tranquil colors of paint on the walls. But if I've caught a fever and I'm feeling sick, or if a nearby faucet has developed a leak, or if a dog in the courtyard six floors below me is barking, the unity of my peaceful scene is spoiled, and comfort flies out the window. And unfortunately, what in fact prevents me more than anything else from feeling really comfortable—whether I'm leaning back against a soft banquette in a pleasant restaurant or spending a drowsy morning in bed propped up on three or four pillows—is actually the well-intentioned ethical training I received as a child.

My parents brought me up to believe in "morality"—an approach toward life that was based on the paradoxical concept of "self-restraint." "Morality" essentially described how a person would behave if he believed all human beings to be equally real, if he cared equally about all human beings, even though one of them happened, in fact, to be himself. And undoubtedly there were certain individuals who had a special gift for morality, the way some people had a gift for music or pleasure. But we, for the most part, lacked that gift, so we were taught principles about how to behave.

And at the same time, we were taught that in order to live morally, it was necessary to seek out accurate knowledge about things. Maybe it could sometimes be "right," for example, to kill another person. But if I acted impulsively and killed another person because of misperceived facts or erroneous suspicions, that would be "wrong."

But I realize now that this entire training in morality is a jarring element in the life I'm leading, and in my struggle to feel comfortable, to feel at ease, it functions rather like a dog whose barking never stops, a dog whose barking persists throughout the day and then continues regularly all night long. It is a perpetual irritation.

Everything visible around me may be perfect and serene, but inside, there is this voice that never stops denouncing me. It does not fit in. Of course I'd be pleased if I could claim that all my relations with other people were in perfect harmony with the laws of morality—and as a matter of fact, in my daily interactions with my friends and colleagues and loved ones, I usually try to follow ethical precepts. But when I draw the curtains of perception a little bit wider and consider the fact that there are thousands and millions of people out there in the world, all quite real, as real as me, and that I have some sort of relation to every one of them, I have to admit that it would be hard to insist that all these relations of mine are truly obedient to those solemn laws.

In contrast to the African miner who works underground doing painfully difficult labor in terrifying conditions and then receives a miniscule reward, I have a life that is extremely pleasant. I have enough money to buy myself warm and comfortable shoes and sweaters; each Wednesday I pay a nice person to clean my apartment and keep it neat; and each April at tax time I pay my government to perform a similar service in the world outside. I pay it to try to keep the world more or less as it is, so that next year it will not suddenly be me who is working a seventy-hour week in some god-forsaken pit or digging in some field under the burning sun. It's all terrific, but my problem is that my government is the medium through which I conduct my relationships with most of my fellow human beings, and I'm obliged to note that its actions don't conform to the principles of morality. Yes, I may be a friendly fellow to meet on the street, but I've found, through my government, a sneaky way to do some terrible things. And so this is why I feel a fantastic need to tear all that moral training out of my heart once and for all so that I can finally begin to enjoy the life that is spread out before me like a marvelous feast. And every time that a friend decides to abandon morality and set himself free, I find that I inwardly exult and rejoice, because it means there will be one less person to disapprove of me if I choose to do the same.

As I write these words, in New York City in 1985, more and more people who grew up around me are making this decision; they are throwing away their moral chains and learning to enjoy their true situation: Yes, they are admitting loudly and bravely, We live in beautiful homes, we're surrounded by beautiful gardens, our children are playing with wonderful toys, and our kitchen shelves are filled with wonderful food. And if there are people out there who are envious of us and who might even be tempted to break into our homes and take what we have, well then, part of our good fortune is that we can afford to pay guards to protect us. And if those who protect us need to hit people in the face with the butts of their rifles, or if they need perhaps even to turn around and shoot, they have our permission, and we only hope they'll do what they do with diligence and skill.

The amazing thing I've noticed about those friends of mine who've made that choice is that as soon as they've made it, they begin to blossom, to flower, because they are no longer hiding, from themselves or anyone else, the true facts about their own lives. They become very frank about human nature. They freely admit that man is a predatory creature, a hunter and a fighter, and they admit that it can warm a human's heart to trick an enemy, to make him cry, to make him do what he doesn't want to do, and even to make him crawl in the mud and die in agony. They admit that to manipulate people can be an art, and that to deceive people can be entertaining. They admit that there's a skill involved in playing life's game, and they admit that it's exciting to bully and threaten and outwit and defeat all the other people who are playing against you. And as they learn to admit these things, and they lose the habit of looking over their shoulders in fear at the disapproaving ghosts of their parents and teachers, they develop the charm and grace that shine out from all people who are truly comfortable with themselves, who are not worried, who are not ashamed of their own actions. These are people who are free to love life exuberantly. They can enjoy a bottle of wine or a walk in the garden with unmixed pleasure, because they feel justified in having the bottle of wine, in having the garden. And if, by chance, they run into the laundress who takes care of their clothes, they can chat with her happily and easily, because they accept the fact that some people, themselves, happen to wear beautiful clothes, and others are paid to keep them clean. And, in fact, these people who accept themselves are people whose company everyone enjoys.

So there are those who live gracelessly in a state of discomfort because they allow themselves to be whipped on an hourly basis by morality's lash, and then there's another group of cheerful, self-confident people who've put morality aside for now, and they're feeling great, and it's fun to be with them. But if we decide that we *don't* need to see all people as equally real, and we come to believe that we ourselves and the groups we belong to are more real, we of course are making a factual mistake.

I was born during World War II, and somehow I've spent a lot of time over the course of my life thinking about the character of Adolf Hitler, and one amazing thing about Hitler was the way his extraordinary self-confidence enabled him to expound his theories of the world to his aides and orderlies and secretaries at the dining room table night after night with no sense that he needed to keep checking to see if his theories were soundly grounded in facts. Hitler's boundless self-confidence enabled him to live each day as a tireless murderer; no weakness, no flagging energy, kept his knife from plunging into his victims hour after hour with mechanical ease.

Hitler was a man who was drawn to murder, to thinking about murder, to dwelling on murder. Particularly to dwelling on murder. Can we not imagine with what eager excitement he must have listened to the reports from the death camps, the crematoria, which he never in fact visited on a single occasion? But when we speak of dwelling on murder…that person standing over the daily newspaper—reading about the massacre, reading about the bloodbath, reading about the execution in a room in the prison—that person is me. And am I not in some part of myself identifying with the one in the story who is firing the machine gun at the innocent people, who is pulling the switch that sends the jolts of power through the prisoner strapped in the electric chair? And do I not also enjoy reading about those incredible scientists who are making the preparations for what we might do in some future nuclear or chemical or biological war that someday might take place? Do I not join them in picturing, with some small relish, the amazing effects that our different devices would have on possible victims? Is my blood not racing with abnormal speed as I read about these things? Is there not something trembling inside me? I know that these planners, these scientists, are not involved in killing. They're killing no one. But I see what they're doing—they're building the gas chambers, getting together the pellets of poison, assembling the rooms where the clothing and valuables will all be sorted, transporting the victims to convenient camps, and asking them to get undressed for the showers and disinfection that will soon follow. Of course, no one is putting people into the chambers. No one is pumping in the gas.

But wait a minute. Am I crazy now? What am I saying? Of course, I may have all sorts of dangerous impulses somewhere inside me, but the difference between Hitler and me is that there was nothing in Hitler that restrained him from following any of his insane impulses to their logical, insane conclusions—he was capable of doing anything at all, if given the chance—because he was utterly without connection to morality.

But I just was thinking about cutting my connection to morality also.

Yes, I was thinking about it. But I didn't do it. At least, I have no memory of doing it. Or was there actually some moment when I did do it, which I've now forgotten?

I don't seem to remember what's happened at all. I know there was a time when I was not like Hitler. The past feels so terribly close. It's as if I could reach out and touch it. Could I have become one of those people who remembers, as if it were yesterday, the time when principles of decency grew freshly in his heart, when a love for humanity set him off on his path in life, who still believes that each of his actions is driven and motivated by those very principles and that very love, but who in fact has become a coarse brute who abandoned love and principles a long time ago?

How could a person break his attachment to morality without noticing it, without feeling it, without remembering it? Could a perfectly decent person just turn into a cold-hearted beast, a monster, and still feel pretty much the same?

Of course. A perfectly decent person can turn into a monster perfectly easily. And there's no reason why he would feel any different. Because the difference between a perfectly decent person and a monster is just a few thoughts. The perfectly decent person who follows a certain chain of reasoning, ever so slightly and subtly incorrect, becomes a perfect monster at the end of the chain.

Thoughts have extraordinary power in the human world, and yet they can behave so unpredictably. Familiar thoughts can lead us by the hand to very strange thoughts. And in a way, we're not as clever as our own thoughts, which have a peculiar habit of developing on their own and taking us to conclusions we never particularly wanted to reach. Within each thought, it seems, other thoughts are hidden, waiting to crawl out.

As the morning begins and I slowly turn my head to look at the clock on my bedside bookcase, my thoughts are already leaping and playing in my brain, ceaselessly spawning other thoughts, changing their shape, dividing in two and then dividing again, merging, dancing together in gigantic clumps. There's no end to the things that the thoughts will do if no one is paying any attention to them.

Our thoughts jump and fly. The world races forward. And meanwhile we're walking slowly around in a daze, trying to remember whether we're still connected to morality or not. False arguments, rapidly expressed, confuse us, seduce us, corrupt us. The chains of reasoning, of thinking, appeared to be sound. What was wrong? But we forget that thinking has its own pathology, and we sit in some room listening to a discussion, and something reasonable and admirable is said, and we nod our heads, and somehow we keep on nodding, and moments later we've agreed to something that would make our former selves turn purple with shame. But we sit there blankly, unaware that anything has happened. Why was it that we failed to notice the first signs of sickness in the argument? At the crucial moment, had our attention wandered? Why would that be? Are we particularly tired right now? Exhausted?

Our lives develop, and our thoughts change, and as our thoughts change, we change. We change each day in small steps, brief conversations, half-conscious moments of reflection, of doubt and resolution.

I stand at the door of my house, ready to defend the loved ones inside from the marauder lurking in the dark. As I steel myself to shoot the marauder, I say to myself, "I must be hard. Cold. Unsentimental." I repeat the litany a hundred times. And the next morning, when the marauder has not come—or the marauder has come, and I have shot him—what do I do with my litany? It doesn't disappear from my mind merely because there is no marauder anymore. Will I adopt it as a permanent creed?

I meet a young woman at a quiet dinner party, and as we sit together she tells me that she sometimes likes to go out with gangsters. She describes in detail the techniques they use in getting other people to do what they want—threats, bribery, violence. I'm shocked and repelled by the stories she tells. A few months later, I run into her again at another party, and I hear more stories, and for whatever reason I don't feel shocked. I'm no longer so aware of the sufferings of those whom the gangsters confront. I'm more impressed by the high style and shrewdness of the gangsters themselves. I begin to understand how difficult it is to be a successful gangster and what extraordinary skill is in fact required to climb to the top of a gangster empire. I find myself listening with a certain enjoyment. By the third time that I encounter this woman I've become a connoisseur of gangster techniques, and the stories she tells now strike me as funny. I consider myself to be, as I always was, a person who entirely disapproves of gangsters, but I still pass on to a friend of mine some of the best stories in the spirit of fun. If my friend now objects that the stories are not really funny, will I find myself somewhat annoyed? Will my friend now seem to me narrow-minded—a humorless bore?

And so every day we encounter the numberless insidious intellectual ploys by which the principle of immorality makes a plausible case for itself, and for every ploy there is a corresponding weakness in our own thinking that causes us not to notice where we're being led until we've already fallen into the trap. Unfortunately, these small intellectual infirmities of ours—our brief lapses of concentration, our susceptibility to slightly inappropriate analogies, the way we tend to forget in what particular contexts the ideas in our heads first made their appearance there, the way our attention can be drawn at the wrong moment by the magician's patter to the hand that does not contain the mysterious coin—just happen to have the power to send history racing off down a path of horror. Morality, if it survived, could protect us from horror, but very little protects morality. And morality, besides, is hard to protect, because morality is only a few thoughts inside our heads. And just as we quickly grow accustomed to brutal deeds and make way before them, so we are quickly stunned into foggy submission by the brutal thoughts which, in our striving for comfort, we have allowed into our minds. And all the time we are operating under the illusion that we, mere individuals, have no power at all over the course of history, when that is in fact (for better or worse) the very opposite of the case.

The shocking truth is that history, too, is at the mercy of my thoughts, and the political leaders of the world sit by their radios waiting to hear whether morality has sickened or died inside my skull. The process is simple. I speak with you, and then I turn out the light, and I go to sleep, but, while I sleep, you talk on the telephone to a man you met last year in Ohio, and you tell him what I said, and then he calls up a neighbor of his, and what I said keeps traveling, farther and farther. And just as a fly can quite blithely and indifferently land on the nose of a queen, so the thought that you mentioned to the man in Ohio can make its way with unimaginable speed into the mind of a president. Because a society, among other things, is a network of brains, and a president is no less involved in his society's network than anyone else, and there is almost nothing that he thinks that doesn't come right from that network. In fact, he is virtually incapable of coming up with an attitude to any problem or to any event that has not been nurtured and developed in that network of brains. When it sooner or later becomes necessary for any of us, whether president or ordinary citizen, to come up with thoughts about political affairs, the only raw materials that we have to draw on are the thoughts we've previously formed—many of them simply thoughts about the conflicts and dramas of our daily lives. Our thoughts may be ones we've acquired from our parents, from our lovers, or from the man in Ohio. But wherever we've found them, they are all we have to work with. Our political attitudes can only come out of what we are—what we learned in school, at the playground, at the office, on the streets, at the party, at the beach, at the dinner table, in bed. And as all of our attitudes flow into action, flow into history, the bedroom and the battlefield soon seem to be one.

My political opinions fly out across the world and determine the course of political events. And political events are determined as well by what I think about the conversation I had with my mother last Saturday when we were having tea. What I say to you about my neighbor's child affects what you feel about the nurse who sits by the side of your friend in the hospital room, and what you say about the nurse affects what your friend's sister thinks about the government of Australia. Everything you are affects me, and everything I am, all my thoughts—the behavior I admire or criticize, the way I choose to spend an hour of my time, the things I like to talk about, the stories I like to hear, the jokes I like to tell—affect the course of history whether I like it or not, whether I know about it or not, whether I care or not. My power over history is inescapable except through death. Privacy is an illusion. What I do is public, and what I think is public. The fragility of my own thoughts becomes the fragility of the world. The ease with which I could become a swine is the ease with which the world could fall apart, like something rotten.

The uncomfortable and incompetent slaves of morality—those awkward, crippled creatures who insist on believing in a standard that condemns them—are less admirable only than those few perfect beings who perhaps obey morality completely. Yes, of course, if we have any sympathy or any affection for people—if we like people—we will be fond of many who treat morality indifferently. But this should not be allowed to confuse us. Morality happens to be a protection that we need in order to avoid total historical disaster, and so, unfortunately, we can't afford to turn our eyes away when our acquaintances, our friends, or we ourselves, drop down a few degrees on the scale of obedience to moral principles. It's obviously foolish and absurd to judge some small decline on the moral scale as if it were a precipitous, lengthy slide, but the temptation is great to be easy on ourselves, and we've all discovered that it's easier to be easy on ourselves if we're all easy on each other too, and so we are. So when a precipitous slide really does take place, a particular effort is required in order to see it. Sophistries, false chains of reasoning, deception, and self-deception all rush in to conceal the fact that any change has occurred at all.

If we live from day to day without self-examination, we remain unaware of the dangers we may pose to ourselves and the world. But if we look into the mirror, we just might observe a rapacious face. Perhaps the face will even show subtle traces, here and there, of viciousness and free-floating hate beneath the surface. All right then, we may say in response to the mirror, we are vile, we know it. Everyone is. That's the way people are.

This self-pitying response to the unflattering news that we're not quite good means that we've decided, if that's how things are, that we'll accept immorality, and we'll no longer make any effort to oppose it.

But it's utterly ridiculous to say that people are vile. If we step outside and pay a brief visit to the nearest supermarket or the nearest café, we'll find ourselves in a position to see, scattered perhaps among scenes of ugliness and greed, examples of behavior that is thoughtful or kind, moments when someone could easily have been cold or cruel but in fact was not. Perhaps we will see the very same person do something harsh and a moment later something gentle. Everyone knows that this element of goodness exists, that it can grow, or that it can die, and there's something particularly disingenuous about extricating oneself from the human struggle with the whispered excuse that it's already over.

FOUR

AN "AMERICAN" PUBLISHES A MAGAZINE

2004

In 2004, in association with Seven Stories Press, I published a magazine called Final Edition *that was designed to have only one issue.*

Most of the writers who appear in this magazine live in New York. We all are "Americans." We all live in the United States. And we have to think about being Americans, because this is a very unusual moment in the history of this country or any country.

A few months ago, the American public, who in political theory and to some extent even in reality are "sovereign" in the United States, were given a group of pictures showing American soldiers tormenting desperate, naked, extremely thin people in chains— degrading them, mocking them, and physically torturing them. And the question arose, How would the American public react to that? And the answer was that in their capacity as individuals, certain people definitely suffered or were shocked when they saw the pictures. But in their capacity as the sovereign public, they did not react. A great public cry of lamentation and outrage did not rise up across the land. The president and his highest officials were not compelled to abase themselves publicly, apologize, and resign, nor did they find themselves thrown out of office, nor did the political candidates from the party out of power grow hoarse with denouncing the astounding crimes that were witnessed by almost everyone alive all over the world. As far as one could tell, over a period of weeks, the atrocities shown in the pictures had been assimilated into the list of things that the American public was willing to consider normal and that they could accept. And so now one has to ask, Well, what does that portend? And so we have to think about being Americans and living in the United States.

To be absolutely frank, the words "the United States" are not interesting to me, and I would much rather think about something else and talk about something else. Life is shockingly short even for those lucky enough to live to be a hundred, and I'd rather fill my brain with, for example, the gorgeous songs called "Book of the Hanging Gardens" by Arnold Schoenberg than with thoughts about men in Washington, D.C., who have a sick need to set fire to cities, wear enormous crowns, and march across crowds of prostrate people. In a way I find those men very, very boring, but the problem is that *they* would say that all of the marching and trampling they're doing is actually for the benefit of me and everyone I know, and unfortunately I have to admit that that actually is true. It's simply true, certainly in regard to me. I lead a very nice, very easy life, thanks to the oil and other supplies that these boring and unappealing men have collected and delivered to my apartment. So I'm up to my neck in being an American, whether I like it or not.

Of course I *don't* like it, because I don't feel a loyalty to this or any other place, apart from our very beautiful planet as a whole. It's not about the United States. Yes, the United States was created through a genocide, but on the other hand the United States has always had some wonderful characteristics. I don't love it, and I don't un-love it. The point is that if things had been left to me, nation-states in general would probably never have been invented. I don't believe in passports or laws on "immigration." I resent going through "Customs and Immigration" at my own country's borders or anyone else's, and I resent the fact that I need anybody's permission to go anywhere, or that anyone does. I don't value an American life more than I value a Nigerian life. I don't think it's more important for an American to have a job than for a Guatemalan to have a job. I just happen to have been born here. That's it. Well, and then I stayed here—in large part because New York City felt actually like a somewhat thrilling microcosm of the world to me—part of one country, part of the United States, yet not really.

In confusing times and bad times, it seems natural to collect around oneself a group of friends and people one trusts, to try to figure things out. So that's what this is. It's not going to be an institution, because I don't understand institutions or usually enjoy them, and in general they might be part of the grandiosity that is part of our problem. So that's why this magazine is going out of business after its first issue and has therefore been given the name *Final Edition.*

FIVE

PATRIOTISM

|99|

In July 1991, the Nation *asked various people to submit brief reflections on "patriotism."*

"Patriotism" can seem to be as harmless as the love of certain musical instruments, food, a landscape. Certain personalities from one's own country can seem so charming, so delightful. But "patriotism" always seems to mean: If you feel a fondness for your country, then it ought to be worth it to you to do "x."

Patriotism is considered to be an emotion a person ought to feel. But why? Why is it nobler to love your own country than to love someone else's? Why is it particularly wonderful to think that the place you're from is the greatest in the world? Why should individuals speak in the first person plural about "our ideals" and "the things we believe"?

If certain great figures from our country's past have had valuable insights, by all means let's be inspired by them. But let's not make a fetish out of it. The United States is a monster that must be stopped, controlled. It's too elaborate to say (again and again), "We must change our current behavior because it violates our noble traditions." The historical point is probably untrue, and anyway, it doesn't matter. What's necessary is to change the behavior. We don't need to be flattered while we're doing it, and in any case, even if we *have* some noble ancestors, that wouldn't mean that *we* have any particular merit.

For citizens of small, weak countries, patriotism might be connected to a yearning for justice. For people who are despised, who despise themselves, more self-esteem might be a good thing. But for people who already are in love with themselves, who worship themselves, who consider themselves more important than others, more self-esteem is not needed. Self-knowledge would be considerably more helpful.

SIX

INTERVIEW WITH NOAM CHOMSKY

2004

September 17, 2004, Noam Chomsky's office in the Department of Linguistics and Philosophy at M.I.T.

Wallace Shawn: A lot of what you've written has to do with the ways in which human beings use their minds—use their very capacity for rationality, one could say—not to seek truth, but on the contrary to distort truth, to twist truth, often so as to justify various crimes they want to commit or have already committed. And this doesn't have to do so much with our personal behavior but with our behavior in groups. So-called leaders dream up the justifications, and everybody else absorbs and accepts them.

Noam Chomsky: It's simply very easy to subordinate oneself to a worldview that's supportive of one's own interests. Most of us don't go around murdering people or stealing food from children. There are a lot of activities that we just regard as pathological when we do them individually. On the other hand, when they're done collectively, they're considered necessary and appropriate. Clinton, Kennedy: they all carried out mass murder, but they didn't think that that was what they were doing—nor does Bush. You know, they were defending justice and democracy from greater evils. And in fact I think you'd find it hard to discover a mass murderer in history who didn't think that…It's kind of interesting to read the Russian archives, which are coming out now. They're being sold, like everything in Russia, and so we're learning something about the internal discussions of the Russian leaders, and they talked to each other the same way they talked publicly. I mean, these gangsters, you know, who were taking over Eastern Europe in the late '40s and early '50s— they were talking to each other soberly about how we have to defend East European democracy from the fascists who are trying to undermine it. It's pretty much the public rhetoric, and I don't doubt that they believed it.

WS: But one has to say about human beings—well, human beings did manage to invent the concepts of truth and falsity, and that's a remarkable accomplishment. And surely if people really used the concepts of truth and falsity rigorously, if they applied the laws of rationality rigorously, they would be forced to confront the true nature of the things they might be planning to do, and that might be enough to prevent them from doing many terrible things. After all, most justifications for mass murder flatly contradict the perpetrator's professed beliefs—and are based on factually false assumptions as well. Couldn't education somehow lead people to use their capacity for rational thought on a more regular basis, to take rationality more seriously? So that they *couldn't* accept absurd justifications for things? As we're sitting here in the Department of Linguistics and Philosophy, wouldn't it benefit the world if more people studied philosophy?

NC: Take Heidegger, one of the leading philosophers of the twentieth century. I mean, just read his straight philosophical work, *An Introduction to Metaphysics*. A few pages in, it starts off with the Greeks, as the origins of civilization, and the Germans as the inheritors of the Greeks, and we have to protect the Greek heritage…This was written in 1935. The most civilized people in the West, namely the Germans—Germany was the most educated country in the world—the Germans were coming under the delusion that their existence, and in fact the existence of Western civilization since the Greeks, was threatened by fierce enemies against whom they had to protect themselves.

I mean, it was deeply imbued in the general culture—in part including German Jews. There's a book by a major humanistic figure of modern Jewish life, Joachim Prinz. He was in Germany in the '30s, and he wrote a book called *Wir Juden* (We Jews), in which he said, Look, we don't like the anti-Semitic undertones of what the Nazis are doing, but we should bear in mind that much of what they're saying is right, and we agree with it. In particular their emphasis on blood and land—*blut und boden*. Basically we agree with that. We think that the identity of blood is very important, and the emphasis on the land is very important. And the tie between blood and land is important. And in fact as late as 1941, influential figures in the Jewish Palestinian community, the pre-state community, including the group that included Yitzhak Shamir, who later became prime minister, sent a delegation to try to reach the German government, to tell them that they would like to make an arrangement with the Germans, and they would be the outpost for Germany in the Middle East, because they basically agreed with them on a lot of things. Now, no one would suggest this was the mainstream, by any means, but it also wasn't a pathological fringe. Or take Roosevelt. Roosevelt was always quite pro-Fascist, thought Mussolini was "that admirable Italian gentleman," as he called him. As late as 1939, he was saying that Fascism was an important experiment that they were carrying out, until it was distorted by the relation to Hitler. And this was almost twenty years after they destroyed the Parliament, broke up the labor movement, raided Ethiopia with all the atrocities…

WS: A lot of people feel that hope for humanity lies not so much in the progress of rationality but rather in the possibility that more people will fall under the influence of moral principles or moral codes, such as the ethical systems developed by various religions. After all, if everyone were seriously committed to moral ideals, then…

NC: Moral codes…you can find things in the traditional religions that are very benign and decent and wonderful and so on, but

I mean, the Bible is probably the most genocidal book in the literary canon. The God of the Bible—not only did he order His chosen people to carry out literal genocide—I mean, wipe out every Amalekite to the last man, woman, child, and, you know, donkey and so on, because hundreds of years ago they got in your way when you were trying to cross the desert—not only did He do things like that, but, after all, the God of the Bible was ready to destroy every living creature on earth because some humans irritated Him. That's the story of Noah. I mean, that's *beyond* genocide—you don't know how to describe this creature. Somebody offended Him, and He was going to destroy every living being on earth? And then He was talked into allowing two of each species to stay alive—that's supposed to be gentle and wonderful.

WS: Hmm…if moral codes themselves can't be relied upon, it's hard to know what to cling to if we want to avoid falling into moral nightmares…In a way, it seems to be simply our obsessive need to have a high opinion of ourselves that leads us repeatedly into idiotic thinking. If our vestigial rationality detects a conflict between our actions and our principles—well, we don't want to change our actions, and it's embarrassing to change our principles, so we wield the blowtorch against our rationality, bending it till it's willing to say that our principles and actions are well-aligned. We're prisoners of self-love.

NC: We understand the crimes of others but can't understand our own. Take that picture over there on the wall. What it is, is the

Angel of Death, obviously. Off on the right is Archbishop Romero, who was assassinated in 1980. The figures below are the six leading Jesuit intellectuals who had their brains blown out in 1989, and their housekeeper and her daughter, who were also murdered. Now, they were murdered by an elite battalion armed, trained, and directed by the United States. The archbishop was murdered pretty much by the same hands. Well, a couple of weeks ago there was a court case in California where some members of the family of Romero brought some kind of a civil suit against one of the likely killers and actually won their case. Well, that's a pretty important precedent, but it was barely reported in the United States. Nobody wants to listen. You know, Czeslaw Milosz was a courageous, good person. And when he died there were huge stories. But he and his associates faced nothing in Eastern Europe like what intellectuals faced in our domains. I mean, Havel was put in jail. He didn't have his brains blown out by elite battalions trained by the Russians. In Rwanda, for about a hundred days they were killing about eight thousand people a day. And we just went through the tenth anniversary. There was a lot of lamentation about how we didn't do anything about it, and how awful, and we ought to do something about other people's crimes, and so on. That's an easy one—to do something about other people's crimes. But you know, every single day, about the same number of people—children—are dying in Southern Africa from easily treatable diseases. Are we doing anything about it? I mean, that's Rwanda-level killing, just children, just Southern Africa, every day—not a hundred days but all the time. It doesn't take military intervention. We don't need to worry about who's going to protect our forces. What it takes is bribing totalitarian institutions to produce drugs. It costs pennies. Do we think about it? Do we do it? Do we ask what kind of a civilization is it where we have to bribe totalitarian institutions in order to get them to produce drugs to stop Rwanda-level killing every day? It's just easier not to think about it.

WS: Totalitarian institutions—you mean the drug companies?

NC: Yes. What are they? The drug companies are just totalitarian institutions which are subsidized: most of the basic research is funded by the public, there are huge profits, and of course from a business point of view it not only makes sense, but it's legally required for them to produce lifestyle drugs for rich Westerners to get rid of wrinkles, instead of malaria treatments for dying children in Africa. It's required. It's legally required.

WS: How do we get out from under that?

NC: Well, the first thing we have to do is face it. Until you face it, you can't get out from under it. Take fairly recent things like the feminist movement—women's rights. I mean, if you had asked my grandmother if she was oppressed she would have said no. She wouldn't have known what you were talking about. Of course she was stuck in the kitchen all day, and she followed orders. And the idea that her husband would do anything around the house…I mean, my mother would not *allow* my father, or me, for that matter, into the kitchen. Literally. Because we were supposed to be studying the Talmud or something. But did they think they were oppressed? Well, actually, my mother already felt that she was. But my grandmother didn't. And to get that awareness—you know, it's not easy.

India is interesting in this respect. There have been some very careful studies, and one of the best was about the province of Uttar Pradesh. It has one of the lowest female to male ratios in the world, not because of female infanticide, but because of the shitty way women are treated. And I mean, I was shocked to discover that in the town where I live, Lexington, which is a professional, upper-middle-class community—you know, doctors, lawyers, academics, stockbrokers, mostly that sort of thing—the police have a special unit for domestic abuse which has two or three 911 calls a week. Now, you know, that's important. Because thirty years ago, they *didn't* have that, because domestic abuse was not considered a problem. Now at least it's considered a problem, and police forces deal with it, and the courts deal with it in some fashion. Well, you know, that takes work—it takes work to recognize that oppression is going on.

This was very striking to me in the student movement in the '60s. I mean, I was pretty close to it, and those kids were involved in something very serious. You know, they were very upset, and they hated the war, and they hated racism, and their choices weren't always the right ones by any means, but they were very emotional about it, for very good reasons…

I was involved particularly with the resisters, who were refusing to serve in the army. They're now called "draft evaders" and so on, but that's bullshit. I mean, almost all of them could have gotten out of the draft easily. A lot of them were theology students, and others—you'd go to your doctor, and he'd say you were a homosexual or something. It was nothing for a privileged kid to get out of the army if he wanted to. They were *choosing* to resist. And facing serious penalties. For an eighteen-year-old kid to go to jail for years or live their life in exile was not an easy choice—especially when, of course, if you conformed, you would just shoot up there and be part of the elite. But they chose it, and it was a courageous decision, and they were denounced for it and condemned for it and so on...At some stage of the game, the feminist movement began. In the early stages of the resistance, the women were supposed to be supportive, you know, to these resisters. And at some stage these young women began to ask, Why are we doing the shit work? I mean, why are we the ones who are supposed to look up in awe at *them*, when we're doing most of the work? And they began to regard themselves as being oppressed. Now that caused a rather serious psychological problem for the boys. Because they thought, and rightly, that they were doing something courageous and noble, and here suddenly they had to face up to the fact that they were oppressors, and that was hard. I mean, I know people who committed suicide. Literally. Because they couldn't face it.

So, just in our lifetime, it's different. The kinds of things that were considered normal—not just normal, unnoticeable, you didn't see them—thirty or forty years ago, would be unspeakable now. The same with gay rights. There have been big changes in consciousness, and they're important, and they make it a better world. But they do not affect *class* issues. Class is a dirty word in the United States. You can't talk about it.

One of my daughters teaches in a state college in which the aspirations of most of the students are to become a nurse or a policeman. The first day of class (she teaches history) she usually asks her students to identify their class background. And it turns out there are two answers. Either they're middle class, or they're [part of the] underclass. If their father has a job, like as a janitor, they're middle class. If their father is in jail or transient, then it's underclass. That's it. Nobody's working class. It's just not a concept that exists. It's not just here—it's true in England too. I was in England a couple of months ago at the time of the Cannes Festival, when Michael Moore won, and one of the papers had a long interview with him, and the interviewer was suggesting that Michael Moore wasn't telling the truth when he said he came from a working-class background. He said he came from a working-class background, but his father had a car and owned a house, so, you know, what's this crap about coming from a working-class background? Well, his father was an auto worker! I mean, the whole concept of class in any meaningful sense has just been driven out of people's heads. The fact that there are some people who give the orders and others who follow them—that is gone. And the only question is, How many goods do you have?—

as if, if you have goods, you have to be middle class, even if you're just following orders.

WS: What you possess determines how people see you and how you see yourself. That defines you—your role in the social structure does not.

NC: People are trained—and massive efforts go into this—people are trained to perceive their identity and their aspirations and their value as people in terms of the things they amass. Nothing else. And in terms of *yourself*, not anyone else…It's kind of interesting to watch this campaign against Social Security going on, and to see the attitudes. I see it even among students. And the reason certain people hate Social Security so much is not just that if you privatize it, it's a bonanza for Wall Street. I'm sure that's part of it, but the main reason for the real visceral hatred of Social Security is that it's based on a principle that they want to drive out of people's heads—namely, that you care about somebody else. You know, Social Security is based on the idea that you care whether the disabled widow on the other side of town has enough food to eat. And you're not supposed to think that. That's a dangerous sentiment. You're supposed to just be out for yourself. And I get this from young people now. They say, Look, I don't see why I should be responsible for her. I'm not responsible for her. I didn't do anything to her. I mean, if she didn't invest properly or, you know, something like that, that's not my business. Why do I have to pay my taxes to keep her alive? And why do I care if the kid down the street can't go to school? I mean, *I* didn't keep him from going to school.

WS: But isn't that sort of demonstrably absurd? I mean, the student who doesn't think he's involved with those other people is simply wrong. He's not a self-created atom. He's a part of society and was created by society. He didn't become whatever he is simply through his own individual efforts. It was society that gave him everything he has and everything he's ever used to become what he is. In order to become what he is, he used the English language, he used the U.S. medical system, electricity, the telephone. He didn't invent the English language. He didn't invent the telephone.

NC: Yes, but people are very deluded about this, including professionals. Take professional economists. Most of them literally believe what Alan Greenspan and others talk about—that the economy flourishes because of entrepreneurial initiative and consumer choice and so on and so forth. You know, that's total bullshit. The economy flourishes because we have a dynamic state sector.

WS: You mean, the motor driving it all is the taxpayer's money being spent—or given away to private companies—by the state. The motor is *not* the individual consumer spending his money in the free market.

NC: Just about everything in the new economy comes out of state initiatives. I mean, what's M.I.T.? M.I.T. is overwhelmingly a taxpayer-funded institution, in which research and development is carried out at public cost and risk, and if anything comes out of it, some private corporation, like the guys who endowed this building, will get the profit from it. And almost everything works like that—from computers, the Internet, telecommunications, pharmaceuticals—you run through the dynamic parts of the economy, that's where they come from. I mean, with things like, say, computers and the Internet, for example, consumer choice had no role at all! Consumers didn't even know these things existed until they'd been developed for years at public expense. But we live in a world of illusion.

WS: People's view of how it's all working is wrong. And of course most people are just totally immersed intellectually in their own personal economic struggle—their struggle to get, basically, things. But you know, when you say that people are trained to focus their aspirations entirely on things—goods—well, that has terrifying implications. To say that people may not even be aware that their lives consist of following orders—that's terrifying. It's as if people don't ac-knowledge that their ability to make choices about their lives, their degree of power over their own environment, is an important issue.

NC: No, what you're taught from infancy is that the only choices you're supposed to make are choices of commodities. It's none of your business how the government works or what government policies are or how the community's organized or anything else. Your job is to purchase commodities.

A lot of it's conscious. There's a conscious strain in sort of liberal, intellectual thought, it goes way back, that the people really don't have any right to participate in the political system. They are supposed to choose among the responsible men.

WS: But it's funny that the people themselves go along with it, because it seems insulting. Why aren't people more insulted? They're not even insulted when they're blatantly lied to! They seem to laugh it off. But in their own lives, in daily life, people would resent it a lot—you know, being lied to.

NC: No—not when people in power lie to you. Somehow there's some law that that's the way it works.

WS: Yes…I feel like saying that your approach to discussing these things is a bit like the approach of a sculptor—with hammer and chisel you attack the big block of marble, and from a certain point of view, all your gestures could be seen as rather hostile or aggressive as you pursue the somewhat negative activity of cutting down the stone, but in the end something rather glorious is revealed. I think you're suggesting that to live in illusion, to be a slave to the worldview of your time and place, or to be all your life a follower of orders—these are all in a way different forms of oppression. But I think you're suggesting that all human beings have the capacity to collaborate in the task of guiding their own lives—and the life of the place where they work, the life of their community, the life of the world. It would be so amazing if people could take that possibility seriously.

SEVEN

BUSH PROPOSES PREEMPTIVE WAR

2002

I was having dinner at a rather expensive restaurant the other night when a man I'd never met before threatened to kill me. He was a distinguished-looking fellow, dressed in a dark suit. I was walking by some appetizing desserts when he approached me, accused me in a harsh voice of bothering him repeatedly, cursed me, and warned that he would kill me if I bothered him again. Then, briskly, he returned to his table. As I went back to my own table in a different part of the restaurant, I mentioned the episode to the maître d', who promised to keep an eye on the guy.

The unpleasant encounter put me in a strange state of mind. I couldn't help noticing, as I looked around the room, that people were coming in, they were being given tables, without any questions being asked by anybody, and within about five seconds of sitting down, they were being issued with weapons that could easily be applied with lethal effect against nearby diners. Wielded with speed, even a fork can kill, not to mention a knife.

After a few moments, though, I calmed down. I felt relatively safe. I finished my meal and even enjoyed it.

The fact was that I was safe from most of the diners, because most of the diners had no desire to kill me. That provided a sort of perfect security, in regard to them. As for the one man who clearly did seem hostile, he was frightening and unpredictable, and his perceptions were inaccurate, but it was still unlikely that he'd try to kill me, because, excitable as he was, he probably knew in some way that threatening me, as he'd done, would cost him absolutely nothing, but that killing me would immediately ruin his life.

As I sit here now, reading the week's newspapers—Iraq, Bush—do I feel safe, or do I feel frightened? Mainly frightened, because we're living in a system of nation-states that is dangerous in and of itself. Like a restaurant, with its uncontrolled, unlicensed population of diners, our world of nation-states is a world of free atoms. Restaurant diners, though, are usually friendly to one another, because they usually belong to the same social group, and restaurants in most places are planted securely inside a system of laws that are designed to provide a quiet life for the dining population.

For all their snarling at one another, nations have so much in common. All of them want to amass weapons. And one way or another, they all come up with some ruler to be on top of them, some boss of some kind who always believes himself to be a reliable custodian of the amassed weapons. Meanwhile, every nation is tortured by its fear of the weapons and the rulers of the other nations. The system is awful! We're all so frightened that we even tell our children frightening stories in school about terrifying rulers, all the

"madmen" throughout history who've tried to "take over the world."
Is there no escape from this?

When the strongest, most successful, and most ruthless person
in a group engages in some particularly nasty and aggressive action
against a weaker member, and then they claim to have done it because of their overpowering fear of that weaker member—well, it's
terribly hard to take them seriously—especially if, instead of looking
frightened, they seem to be excited. But assuming, for the sake of argument, that Bush really wants to preemptively attack Iraq because
of genuine fear, then one has to say that this doesn't make sense.

Bush claims to be frightened by Iraq. But it's the restaurant that's
dangerous, not one diner. Heavily armed or not, Iraq is unlikely to attack either our country or any other country, for the very same reason
that the man in the restaurant didn't attack me—fear of the consequences. The man was isolated and weak in the face of society's legal
system. Iraq is a small impoverished nation in comparison to any
country it might be tempted to attack.

Bush indeed recognizes the danger inherent in a world divided
up into armed fiefdoms. His proposed solution is that one of those
fiefdoms, his own, should become more powerful than any of the
others and should preserve peace, order, and stability by attacking
any fiefdom whose ruler is potentially hostile.

The flaw in this proposed solution is that Bush's fiefdom, the
Unites States, will inevitably face many hostile rulers. This is not
just a possibility—it's a certainty, because in the world as it is, most

people are degraded for the benefit of the few, and the few happen to include Bush, his friends, and the privileged elite of the United States. The stability Bush hopes to enforce, personally, is known by everyone to benefit him, personally, and the more he identifies himself as the enforcer, the more hostility will be focused on him and on the United States.

If he responds to this hostility by attacking what by definition will be under his proposal much weaker nations, his use of violence, his sowing of destruction and death among the less powerful, will arouse even greater hostility, and more and more fiefdoms around the world will come to be headed by rulers who hate our nation. In other words, Bush's proposed plan for preventing any possible threats against us, a plan that amounts in practice to an attempt to "take over the world," can only end in greater and greater isolation for the United States—and ultimately, in the long term, in some sort of military defeat.

EIGHT

THE INVASION OF IRAQ
IS MOMENTS AWAY

2003

Fragments from a Diary

January

New Year's Eve—so quiet—unlike any New Year's Eve that I can remember. Even people who usually have three or four parties to go to were invited nowhere or purposely decided to stay in. We stayed in too. We were falling asleep when big bangs and odd screaming seemed to announce that midnight had come.

In the cold weather, in New York, in January of 2003, everyone is frozen.

We're passengers. We're waiting. We're sitting very quietly in our seats in the car, waiting patiently for the driver to arrive. We're nervous, of course, looking out the window at the gray landscape. Soon the driver will open the door, sit down in his seat, and take us on a trip. We're going to Iraq. We don't want to go. We know we'll be driving straight into the flames, straight ahead into the flames of hell. It's crazy. It's insane. We know that. But we're paralyzed, numb, can't seem to move. Don't seem to know how to reason with the driver. Don't seem to know how to stop the car from going. Don't seem to know how to get out of the car.

◆　　　◆　　　◆

How fascinated people are—in every country!—by the special little men they call their "leaders." What a terrible way to live.

Here, we think about our leaders all the time. We dream about them. It wasn't so many centuries ago that kings and emperors were remote from their subjects. Their subjects didn't even know what their faces looked like. But I'm as familiar with the face of Richard Cheney or of Donald Rumsfeld as I am with the faces of my closest friends.

Our enormous country is really a tiny principality, in which our leaders loom gigantically large in the quiet green landscape. Here in our country, our sky is actually not a sky, it's a specially designed impenetrable dome, and inside it we're calmed by soothing music and soothing voices. Every morning we're given our *New York Times*, which teaches us to see our leaders "as people." Our newspaper helps us to get to know our leaders, their quirks, their personalities, helps us really to identify with them. I understand their problems, what they're trying to do, how difficult it is. And I share a life with them— at least I share the essential things: a climate sweetened by electricity, warm in winter, cool in summer; armchairs, bathrobes, well-made boots, pleasant restaurants. Just like our leaders, I like the old songs of

Frank Sinatra, I like to watch Julia Roberts in the movies, I like driving quietly through the fall foliage in New England, I like lemon
meringue pie and banana splits. Our leaders share my life, and they've
made my life. I *have* my life because of them. Can that be denied? Is
my life of pasta and pastries and books and concerts not based on the
United States being the mighty nation they insist it should be?

◆   ◆   ◆

Like Richard Cheney's life and Donald Rumsfeld's life, my life
is set in motion by those poor crushed fossils under the sand of
Saudi Arabia and the sand of Iraq. The price of the fossils must stay
cheap. The boys are going to be fighting this war with money from
my taxes, and they're going to bring me back the prize—my own
life. Yes, I'm involved, to put it mildly.

The experience of following "the news" each day before an enormous event occurs, as now before (maybe) war, reminds me of an old
sensation: There was a children's game in which we were supposed to
pin a paper tail on a paper donkey, and before you made your attempt
you were blindfolded, and invisible hands spun you around and
around till you were dizzy and disoriented and didn't know where you
were. I remember it so well! That's how I feel. President Bush is about
to take a step toward seizing control of the entire planet. People and
countries are terrified about the consequences for the human race if
Bush does what he plans to do. And yet it seems as if we, the consumers of "news," when we try each day to learn about this desperately

important moment we're living through, are given a huge, overpowering pile of stories, almost all of which deal not with the question of humanity's future, but instead with the question of Iraq's weapons.

Bush himself is not thinking about the weapons held (or not held) by this destroyed country, Iraq, nor is he actually shocked by the probability that Iraq, like all the other nations on earth (because of the nature of "nations"), wants to be as well armed as it possibly can be. But he's managed to convince the governments of the world that, just as he will never say why he actually wants to invade Iraq but will only talk about Iraq's weapons, *they* must never say why they *oppose* the invasion, except by talking about Iraq's weapons. Bush will say Iraq has a lot of weapons, the opponents of war will say Iraq has few. This discussion will go on until the troops are ready and the weather's right for war, and at that moment Bush will declare he's "lost patience" with the laborious pace of the discussion of weapons, and he'll go to war.

The editors of the *New York Times* must know as well as anyone else that the discussion of weapons is the public relations branch of preparing for war, the propaganda arm of the process of preparation. The discussion of weapons, on Bush's part, is not sincere, and it only makes sense when seen as part of the story of preparation. But each morning I find in my newspaper two separate narratives, apparently describing unrelated developments: one (a thin little column) says that the preparations for war are going smoothly and the weather soon will be right for an attack, and the other (pages and pages) says that the negotiations about Iraq's weapons are going poorly, and there's a danger that Bush may "lose patience." The thin column describes something that's actually happening. The pages and pages spin me around until I don't know where I am.

February

We've marched in Washington and then in New York. The protests around the world are astonishing! The despair we felt earlier is melting fast. In fact, our mood has utterly changed. But we have to ask, has Bush's mood changed?

◆   ◆   ◆

In school we were taught various terms to characterize political systems—"oligarchy," "autocracy," "democracy." What is our system? No term for it exists. To call it a democracy seems so wrong. How can you call it a democracy when, for example, still today the public is not aware that in 1991 the first President Bush circumvented quite plausible opportunities to avoid war with Iraq? Yes, we're allowed to vote for our leaders, but we're not allowed to know what they're like, because we're not allowed to know what they do. The enormous enterprises of the government are conducted sometimes for the benefit of certain citizens, maybe even sometimes for the benefit of all of them, but the citizens don't even know what the government is doing, much less who the beneficiaries are. The citizens can hardly

be expected to have intelligent opinions on the government's decisions, because the citizens don't know what's actually going on, and
they can't find out. At the appropriate moments, we're brought in to
cheer, but we've never been told what actually happened.

Sometimes a man like Jimmy Carter may blunder into the
White House and sit down behind the desk in the Oval Office, and
the rules of the system have to be explained to him. Jimmy Carter
declared that he would "never lie" to the public. This was like a new
man being selected as CEO of General Foods and announcing that
from now on he planned to bake every General Foods cookie himself in his own kitchen. It didn't take long to teach Carter the ropes.

You can say that Bush and his colleagues would like to conquer
Iraq in order to possess a secure source of oil and to begin a process of
controlling the world, but that may not fully account for the strength
of their motivation, the evident fervor of their commitment.

Why are we being so ridiculously polite? It's as if there were
some sort of gentlemen's agreement that prevents people from stat-
ing the obvious truth that Bush and his colleagues are exhilarated
and thrilled by the thought of war, by the thought of the incredible
power they will have over so many other people, by the thought of
the immensity of what they will do, by the scale, the massiveness of
the bombing they're planning, the violence, the killing, the blood,
the deaths, the horror.

The love of killing is inside each one of us, and we can never be
sure that it won't come out. We have to be grateful if it *doesn't* come

out. In fact, it is utterly wrong for me to imagine that Bush is violent and I am not, that Bush is cruel and I am not. I am potentially just as much of a killer as he is, and I need the help of all the sages and poets and musicians and saints to guide me onto a better path, and I can only hope that the circumstances of my life will continue to be ones that help me to stay on that path. But we can't deny that Bush and his men, for whatever reason, are under the sway of the less peaceful side of their natures. From the first days after the World Trade Center fell, you could see in their faces that, however scary it might be to be holding the jobs they held, however heavy the responsibility might be for steering the ship of state in such troubled times, they in fact were loving it. Those faces glowed. You could see that special look that people always have when they've just been seized by that most purposeless of all things, a sense of purpose. This, combined with a lust for blood, makes for particularly dangerous leaders, so totally driven by their desire for the violence to start that they're incapable of hearing any voices around them who plead for compromise or peace.

Why do they want this war so much? Maybe we can never fully know the answer to that question. Why do some people want to be whipped by a dominatrix? Why do some people want so desperately to have sex with children that they can't prevent themselves from raping them, even though they know that what they're doing is wrong? Why did Hitler want to kill the Jews? Why do some people collect coins? Why do some people collect stamps?

We can't fully understand it. But it's clear that Bush and his group are in the grip of something. They're very far gone. Their narcissism and sense of omnipotence goes way beyond self-confidence, reaching the point that they're impervious to the disgust they provoke in others, or even oblivious to it. They've made very clear to the people of the world that they value American interests more than the world's interests and American profits more than the world's physical health, and yet they cheerfully expect the people of the world to accept the wisdom of their leadership in the matter of Iraq. They're so unshakable in their belief that everyone will admire them that they happily summoned the world, a year ago, to look at enlarged photographs of what they'd done to people they'd taken as prisoners, proudly exhibiting them on their knees in cages, under a ferocious sun, with their faces hooded and their bodies in chains. In other words, the only thing you can really say about these men is that like all of those who for fifty years have sat in offices in Washington and dreamed of killing millions of enemies with hydrogen bombs, these people have become sort of crazy. They have an illness.

Meanwhile, I read my *New York Times*, and it's all very calm. The people who write in its pages seem to have a need to believe that their government, while sometimes somewhat wrong, of course, can't be *entirely* wrong, and must at least be trusted to raise the right questions. These writers just can't bear the thought of being completely alienated from the center of their society, their own government. Thus—although they themselves, if they'd been asked about it two years ago, would have called a "preemptive" invasion of Iraq an insane and absurd proposition—they must now take the idea very seriously and weigh its merits respectfully and worry gravely about the dangers posed by Iraq, even though Iraq is in no way more dangerous than it was two years ago, and in every possible way it is less dangerous.

In fact, the dispassionate tone of the "debate" about Iraq in the *New York Times* and on every television screen seems psychotically remote from the reality of what will happen if war actually occurs. We are talking about raining death down on human beings, about thousands and thousands of howling wounded human beings, dismembered corpses in pools of blood. Is this one of the "lessons of Vietnam" that people have learned—that the immorality of this unspeakable murdering must never be mentioned? That the discussion of murder must never mention murder, and that even the critics of murder must always criticize it because it is not in the end in our own best interest? Must the critics always say that the murders would come at too high a price for *us*, would be too expensive, would unbalance our budget, hurt our economy, cause us to spend less on domestic priorities; that it would lose us our friends, create enemies for us? Can we never say that this butchering of human beings is horrifying and wrong?

Yesterday I walked through a neighborhood of shabby apartment buildings on shabby streets, and I ate lunch in a lousy restaurant. The bread was hard, and the lettuce was rather stiff as well. But to tell you the truth, the experience wasn't that bad. I could survive some lousiness, some uncomfortableness, some decline. Back on the street, I kept walking for a while and wondered what would happen if we allowed some of the fossils to simply lie there under the sand, if we decided not to try to dominate the world. We'd have no control over what would happen. We'd let go and fall. How far would we sink? How far? How far? Sure, it's been great, the life of comfort, good lunches, predictability. But imagine how it would feel if we could be on a path of increasing compassion, diminishing brutality, diminishing greed—I think it might actually feel wonderful to be alive.

NINE

UP TO OUR NECKS IN WAR

2004

Fragments from a Diary

Early September

It's tragic when civilians die in war. But is it really less tragic when soldiers die? Why do people tally the deaths of Iraqi and Afghan civilians—but leave Iraqi and Afghan soldiers out of the accounting? Did the soldiers in those miserable armies deserve to die? Because they were soldiers? These were just young men—some were conscripted against their will, others decided to risk their lives and enlist (maybe because they were desperate, because they were ignorant, because they loved their country). Please don't tell me they deserved to be massacred and not even counted.

Who does "deserve to die"? Whose death should not be mourned? Some say: the guilty deserve to die and should not be mourned.

◆　　◆　　◆

We all belong to the same species—and yet…A farmer wakes

up in the morning and says, "I hope I can plant the seeds today before it starts to rain." An artist wakes up in the morning and says, "I hope I can paint a good picture." But those who control arsenals of weapons wake up quite differently. George Bush wakes up in the morning, looks at himself in the mirror, and says, "I'll kill people today." Osama bin Laden wakes up and says, "I'll kill people today." They believe they're gods, that it's appropriate for them to wield power over life and death. They believe that the ones they will kill are guilty of crimes and deserve to die.

To Bush, an Afghan farmer who fought for the Taliban is guilty of a crime, because that farmer helped to support the government of his country, which helped a man, bin Laden, who inspired people who killed Americans. To bin Laden, a secretary working in an office at the World Trade Center was guilty of a crime because she worked for a corporation that was a part of a system of international capitalism that supported a status quo in the world in which Muslims are oppressed.

Of course there are particular instances in which even hardened killers find it too absurd to claim that that their chosen victims are guilty of crimes and deserve their deaths. This is particularly the case when the victims are children. In those cases—the Chechen rebels' killing of child hostages, Bill Clinton's imposition of child-killing sanctions on Iraq—the claim is simply that the absolute necessity of achieving the goal (the liberation from Russian oppression, the hostile leverage that Clinton wanted to apply to Saddam Hussein's regime) turns the killing of the innocent into an appropriate tactic.

A lot of hypocrisy comes into play in discussions about killing.

I believed in the Sandinista Revolution in Nicaragua, although it was led by people who took it upon themselves to kill in order to achieve their purpose. I rejoiced at the end of apartheid, although it wouldn't have ended if it hadn't been for the actions of the African National Congress, which took it upon itself to kill in order to end apartheid. When you live in a place where oppression is murdering your countrymen, where people are cold and have no shelter, where people are hungry, where people are starving, where people's lives are being crushed by the status quo, you may feel a desperate need to take immediate action, and the human imagination is only rarely capable of devising and embracing a Gandhian approach to the necessary confrontation with the ruling powers. So at times a simple choice appears to exist between the human death daily caused by the existing system and the use of death-creating force to effect change. And to denounce all of those whose battle for change has not excluded violent methods may be to condemn most people on earth to inevitable suffocation. There may always indeed be a third, nonviolent path, but it's usually the hardest path to see. Yes, if I'm involved, I must struggle to find it, but I can't bring myself to condemn Nelson Mandela and everyone else whose principled struggle for justice fell short of the nonviolent ideal.

Nonetheless, I always come back to the feeling that it's basically sickening for an individual to decide about himself, "Yes, my cause is just, and so I grant myself the power over life and death, I grant myself the right to decide who will live and who will die, I grant myself the right to kill the guilty, I grant myself the right to kill the innocent."

Killing other people is a terrible thing, and everyone knows it. So those who have killed are highly motivated to explain and defend what they've done, with the result that for every bullet shot out into the world, you might say that a page of explanation suddenly floats down into the world as well, adding to the enormous world-file of explanations, many hypocritical.

Those who embark on a program of killing may offer explanations using direct phrases or indirect phrases. George Bush's phrase "the war on terror" reduced Bush's individual enemies to a generalized abstraction, as if Osama bin Laden and all Muslims who violently oppose the actions of the United States are so profoundly immoral and alien that they can't even be confronted as human beings but can only be seen as a swarm of creatures to be exterminated—creatures whom we imagine to be unable even to understand human speech, creatures with whom communication simply is not possible.

To call the attitude behind Bush's concept of "the war on terror" hypocritical is simply to say: Yes, it *is* hard to believe that any human beings could be so inhuman as to crash planes into the World Trade Center, but it also happens to be hard to believe that any human beings could massacre the defenseless Zulus, entire families, as the British did in the days of the empire, or rape and murder innocent islanders, as the Japanese did in World War II, or systematically, relentlessly drop explosives and napalm from gleaming airplanes onto peasant villages, year after year, as the Americans did in the Vietnam War.

The Americans happen to have destroyed the city of Hiroshima with an atomic bomb, so Americans who pretend to be shocked by the vileness of Osama bin Laden are living in some sort of fantasy world. Bin Laden and his followers have a point of view for which they're willing to kill—in other words, they're just like the others, they're like us. Some of what bin Laden thinks is perfectly reasonable. Like Paul Wolfowitz, like Pat Robertson, like Ariel Sharon, like George Bush, bin Laden thinks a lot of things that are *not* reasonable.

Bin Laden is admired by many Muslims. Some clearly admire him because of his least reasonable beliefs. But many admire him because they feel there's something terribly wrong with the circumstances in which they live, and bin Laden's anger symbolizes for them a desire for a better life. And that desire is not at all unreasonable.

Late September—Autumn Begins

Not unlike those unfortunate individuals who have somehow become addicted to pornography on the Internet, a frightening number of Americans seek temporary relief in nationalistic fantasy from the unsatisfying incompleteness of their daily lives—and then become hooked. It's been going on for years. Their particular dream is not about sex or pleasure, it's not even a dream about beautiful fields or ocean waves—it's a dream about blood that flows from the wounds of the enemies of the nation. And just as the male heterosexual pornography addict identifies with, and revels in, the exploits of the triumphant naked male in the pornographic scene, the American nationalism addict identifies with the soldier, the bomber, and above all with the president. The end of the Cold War was a moment of anxiety for the American nationalism addict. Pornography privileges were suddenly withdrawn. The apparently implacable Soviet leaders, sitting perennially in a row in their uncomfortable-looking uniforms and suits, disappeared from the television screens, along with the trudging, raggedy armies of "Marxist guerrillas" in various countries around the world, and so, just as ex-alcoholics (like President Bush) are nonplussed or worse by the sudden disappearance of their necessary substance, nationalism addicts in the 1990s experienced serious depression if not desperation. But in 2001, the emergence of "the terrorists" finally brought relief. In fact, "the terrorists" were an improvement, as the Russians had never actually attacked the United States, nor had their statements expressed visceral loathing against us.

One of the peculiarities of heterosexual pornography made for men is that so much screen time is given to the penis, and one of the peculiarities of nationalistic fantasy is that so much of the dream is about the wonderfulness of the national self as the blows are being struck, while little curiosity is directed to the characteristics of the bleeding victim/enemy. The mental camera focuses on the noble intentions and plans of the slaughterer, while the supposedly once-dangerous victim offers up blood and cries but apparently possesses no intentions, thoughts, or feelings at all.

The eighteenth-century figures who devised the theory of modern democracy, not to mention the ancient Greeks, had something else in mind. The American theorists thought that citizens would live and vote based on a rational consideration of their own interests. A political speech might, in the imagination of these practical philosophers, convince its listeners through a persuasive marshalling of evidence and inferences. But to put a drug into someone's drink, knock them out, and carry them home is not a form of seduction, and to paralyze a listener's brain with fantasy—whether injected by a needle through the skull or poured into the ears through the spoken word—is not a form of rational argument, nor any basis for what those theorists would have called "democracy."

Residents of mental institutions are not usually brought by their keepers to the voting booth on Election Day. They fall too far short of the image of the citizen/voter that inspired the authors of the Federalist Papers. And yet people whose brains are pickled in fantasy—people whose knowledge of the real world outside their own neighborhood (or even within it) may be close to nonexistent—are allowed to vote.

The American citizen's vote is a powerful weapon. The election of Ronald Reagan, the election of Bill Clinton, was, for various individuals across the planet, an inescapable portent foretelling their death. But the great majority of the voting American citizens cast their ballots without an awareness of those individuals and the terrifying destiny hidden inside their act of voting.

If one imagines a system in which Smith and Jones are running for office, but voters must cast their ballots only for "Candidate A" or "Candidate B" without being allowed to know which candidate is Smith and which is Jones, you could say, assuming the votes are honestly counted, that the voters do determine the outcome of the election, but as citizens they have no power. When they vote, they're participating in a ritual, like kowtowing before an emperor.

If American voters don't know the meaning of their own votes and float into the voting booth drugged with fantasies, their act of voting is only a ritual. But apparently this doesn't bother the voters, and it doesn't bother the press or the politicians either.

Newspapers and networks are commercial enterprises whose goal is basically to win large audiences by entertaining people and pleasing them. Politicians also are trying to please—they're trying to win votes by presenting themselves attractively and by telling the public a flattering story about itself. They too adopt the concerns of the professional showman whose goal is to be liked. And just like the commercial journalist, the political candidate has no desire to alienate the potentially defensive and self-protective audience by suddenly revealing that their treasured myths are nothing but lies. Thus, in our current American election season, the public can hear from the Republican candidate (who believes it) and from the Democratic candidate (who is consciously lying) that the Vietnam War was an honorable struggle by the United States, and "the terrorists" attacked in 2001 because they were "filled with hate" for no reason at all. Of course various well-meaning candidates may hope to "return" to the path of truth once their expedient deceits have paved the way to their political success. But that's a dangerous game. Every convincing lie increases the confidence of the one who believes it that his current view of life is indeed correct, which will make it harder, at any time in the future, to persuade that person that his view is wrong. And if circumstances change, and the liar would like to take back his lie, it may not be possible to do so without running the risk that everyone will know he was lying earlier, and so he becomes obliged to act as if what he once knew to be true had somehow become false.

And so the real battles are fought between ruling elites, and the voters, the citizens, are just a semiconscious prey for whoever is drugging them. And this is quite dangerous for the dazed citizens. This is why democracy was invented in the first place. It's very pleasant to be entertained, but if the audience isn't looking out for its own welfare, it might not survive. Who will help it? Who will warn it of danger? The one who provides the entertainment? Unfortunately, the entertainer can't be trusted to do that. The entertainer is paid to do a different job. Of course, to tell pleasing falsehoods to a blind man or woman in a dangerous environment is admittedly not very nice—but the long-term welfare of the audience is just not the entertainer's concern.

TEN

ISRAEL ATTACKS GAZA

DECEMBER 2008

Jews, historically, have been irrationally feared, hated, and killed, and it's not surprising that the irrationality that has surrounded them for so many centuries, the fire of irrationality in which they were almost extinguished, has jumped across from soul to soul, as if in a folktale or myth, and taken possession of many Jews, in Israel and in the United States.

Recent history shows that the Jews, as a people, have found few friends who are honest and true. During World War II, when Hitler's anti-Semitism was murdering Jews by the million, the world's nations expressed their own anti-Semitism by refusing to house and welcome the tortured people, preferring instead to let them be exterminated if need be. After the war, the world felt it owed the Jews something—but then showed its lack of true regard for the tormented group by "giving" them a piece of land already populated (and surrounded) by another people—an act of European imperialism carried out exactly at the moment when non-European peoples all over the world were finally concluding that European imperialism was completely unacceptable and had to be resisted. And now we have the spectacle of American politicians encouraging and financing Israeli policies which will ultimately lead to more disaster and destruction for Jews.

It is not rational to believe that the Palestinians in the Occupied Territories will be terrorized by force and violence, by cruelty, by starvation, or by slaughter into a docile acceptance of the Israeli occupation. There is no evidence that that could possibly happen, and there are mountains of evidence to the contrary.

Many Israelis and many American Jews clearly believe that the Jews have always had enemies and always will have enemies—and who can be shocked that certain Jews might think that? To some of these individuals, a Palestinian boy throwing stones at an Israeli soldier, even if the boy's house has been destroyed by the Israeli army, even if his family has been killed by them, is simply one figure in an eternal mob of anti-Semites, a mob made up principally of people to whom the Jews have done no harm at all, as they did no harm to Hitler. The conclusion drawn by many who hold this view of the world is that in the face of such massive and eternal opposition, Jews are morally justified in taking any measures they can think of to protect themselves. They are involved in one long eternal war, and a few hundred Palestinians killed today must be measured against many millions of Jews who were killed in the past. The agony the Israelis might inflict on a Palestinian family today must be seen in the perspective of Jewish families in agony all over the world in the past.

It is irrational for the Israeli leaders to imagine that the Palestinians will understand this particular point of view—will understand why Jews might find it appropriate, let us say, to retaliate for the death of one Jew by killing a hundred Palestinians. If a Palestinian killed a hundred Jews to retaliate for the killing of one Palestinian—for that matter, if a Thai killed a hundred Cambodians to retaliate for the killing of one Thai—the Israeli leaders of course would agree that that would be unjust, that would be racist, as if one Palestinian or one Thai were worth a hundred Israelis or a hundred Cambodians. But if a Jew kills a hundred Palestinians to retaliate for the killing of one Jew, to many Israelis this does not seem unjust, because it's part of an eternal struggle in which the Jews have lost and lost and lost—they've already lost more people than there are Palestinians. Well, it's not surprising that certain Jews would feel this way, but no Palestinian will ever share that feeling or be willing to accept it. What the Palestinians see is an implacable and heartless enemy, one that considers itself unbound by any rules or principles—an enemy that can't be reasoned with but can only be feared, hated, and if possible killed.

As the years go by, and the Holocaust fades farther into the past, in every country more and more people are born to whom the outrageous behavior of the Israelis seems simply hateful, and to whom justifications based in the past seem simply sophistical. In particular, poor and oppressed people around the world are very well aware of the events in the Occupied Territories. They know little about the history of the Jews, and they identify strongly with the Palestinian struggle and point of view. During the period of time in which these younger people have been alive, the Jews have not been, for the most part, persecuted victims. They've seemed like unusually self-righteous victimizers. In other words, Israeli policy is day by day stoking a rage against Israel that can only lead to a grim future for all Israelis and possibly for all Jews everywhere.

Consequently, it's patronizing and disgraceful and no favor to the Jews for American politicians—for narrow, short-term political advantage, for narrow, short-term global/strategic reasons, or even because of a sense of guilt over past Jewish suffering—to pander to the irrationality of the most irrational Jews.

PART TWO

DREAM-WORLD

ELEVEN

MYSELF AND HOW I GOT INTO THE THEATRE

1996

I would love to say something useful about my plays. Unfortunately, the only thing that really seems to connect them is the fact that "I" wrote them—and I've always had a very very hard time trying to define or understand the word "I" and the concept of the self. If the self is defined as the personality, then it seems relevant to say that the plays I've written don't particularly seem to reflect the person I know myself to be (or think myself to be)—except perhaps insofar as I may have decided to rearrange myself to conform to them after the fact. But if I'm going to say something about how my plays came to have the particular qualities they have, where else can I begin but with some biographical hints?

I grew up in New York City, and as I suppose anyone can tell in two seconds if they meet me, I am what people call a "child of privilege." This is the defining fact about me, and it always will be, and if I live to be two hundred years old, I'll never be able to erase the traces of it. Like everyone else who comes from that particular tribe, the children of the privileged, I was brought up to believe in the central belief of the tribe: that there's a certain (large) quantity of the world's fruits that is the appropriate portion of the children of the privileged. But I came from a family that was a "liberal" family, so, rather confusingly, I was encouraged to feel that for every dollar I took from the world, I really ought (for some reason) to "give back" a penny, at least a penny's worth of something. The unspoken and (in the case of my parents, certainly) un-thought belief of the liberal privileged group was that one was supposed to be ready to rob and murder in order to secure one's appropriate portion, but as one rode off from the conquest one was always to remember to toss back to the victims a small offering, a small scrap torn off from what one had just taken.

Our family was privileged, but it was carefully explained to me that we were not rich, only "middle class," and so, oddly, I would need to "work for my living" rather than just receiving it automatically—in other words, the little package that was the life I'd inevitably possess would be waiting for me in the baggage room with my name written on it, but, annoyingly, it wouldn't be delivered to the house, I'd have to get into a taxi and go get it.

Despite this, I grew up lazy, and I've stayed lazy. I've always liked to eat ice cream and cake, and the line of least resistance for me has always been close to the border of sleep. When I was nine or ten, I kept an enormous mound of comic books on the floor of my bedroom, and my favorite thing was to burrow into my mound, find myself a comfortable position there, and in this wonderful swamp, which was also readable, I would reach a state that fell exactly midway between reading and napping.

As far as my connection to other people went, I was usually affectionate. I was usually fond of the people I met: the privileged. And I'm still fond of them. I know them well. It's easy for me to see them not as others might see them, as a group of people who fundamentally are all the same, because as holders of privilege they all play fundamentally the same social role, but as they see themselves: as remarkably distinct individuals with different opinions, thoughts, and characteristics. I know very well that they suffer, I know that they're lonely, they're lost, they're desperate, whatever.

On the other hand, there's always been some small element in me that is a bit less lazy and a bit less affectionate. You could say, boringly, that I've therefore often been a "person in conflict."

I've always loved making things, shaping things. I've always loved colored pencils and puppets and imaginary landscapes. The experience of inventing people and places, thinking about which phrase best expresses a thought, is more than enough to fill a lifetime for me. But occasionally my absorption in these voluptuous pleasures is interrupted by what one might compare in some ways to the pain of the amputee's severed limb—a weird memory of the people to whom I seem to have no current connections: the poor and the oppressed. Perhaps it was my father, who taught me to love art, who also in some way nourished these perverse "memories." I remember once, when I was ten or so, I was riding with him in a taxi and I drew his attention to an overweight, bizarre, rather miserable-looking boy whom we were passing in the street. I found the boy funny and was merrily laughing away at him when I turned around and was shocked to discover that my poor father had burst into tears. The sight of the boy hadn't struck him as funny, apparently, and my response to the boy had also, apparently, not made him happy.

Well, I guess you can see that a young man can't go too long without writing about his father. In any case, I will tell you about mine that he happened to be, of all things, an editor, a kind and beloved mentor to writers, and at the same time a highly respected judge of literature; and whenever my father was discussed, and it was really very often, it was always said that he had "high standards." (I mean, other people said it; God knows he never would have, because it would have seemed to him horribly pompous, and because he would have found the metaphor ridiculous and incoherent—one pictures with difficulty someone measuring something somehow with some odd device while standing on a ladder.) Unfortunately, in contrast to my father, I never really comprehended the whole concept of measuring in the first place. If *I* listened to a piece of music, saw a film, or read a book—well, I seemed to go through it all from moment to moment, somehow. I was enlightened or confused, indifferent or thrilled, and certain things were offered to me that I needed, or didn't, and then it was over, and I couldn't really remember the piece of work as a whole, much less pass judgment on it. In a way I didn't *see* the piece of work at all—I just lived inside it for a while or something. So when people said that the music or the book or the film was "good" or "bad," I usually felt that I just didn't know what they were talking about.

At the liberal schools to which my parents had sent me, judgment was not part of the daily routine. The schools proudly boasted that they gave no grades or marks, and so we ourselves were never judged or condemned; there was no "good" or "bad," the point was just to do what interested you, and that was something I could understand well. All the same, my father, at home, gentle as he was, would sometimes say of some piece of writing that had crossed his desk that it "hadn't worked out"; and yes, he even described certain people's attempts as "mistakes." And how was I supposed to deal with that? Well, I must say I didn't like the sound of those comments at all. No, it made me feel quite uncomfortable to hear comments like that, particularly as I began to feel that I might someday become a writer myself. After all, it was clear enough even to me that, just as a dancer might fall down during a performance, or a pianist might hit a bunch of wrong notes in a difficult passage, well, there were certain things in the field of poetry, say, certain things that an ignorant apprentice might very well write, which an accomplished master would *not* write, and there were people who actually could tell the difference, and my father was one of them. I couldn't simply dismiss the sorts of judgments my father passed. On the other hand, I honestly couldn't face being subjected to them.

Which brings me to the question of how I got into writing for the theatre. Well, it was not just that theatre happened to be the only branch of literature that my father personally stayed entirely away from; it was more that I could easily sense in some half-conscious way—and in New York in the late '60s, when I first started writing, it was particularly easy to sense this—I could sense that the whole field of theatre was really a strange sort of non-field, in which the whole business of "standards" just didn't apply. Theatre was a kind of void, a blank, an undefined emptiness. Because, I mean, what *is* theatre, really?

Is theatre an "art form"? Is drama an "art"? Poetry is an art. Painting is an art. But can a play seriously be compared to a poem or a painting? Can you seriously claim that a play can be compared to a string quartet? Well, certain playwrights have actually believed that theatre is an artistic field: Maeterlinck, for example, whose works I always loved, created aesthetically satisfying self-contained worlds, entirely distinct from the world we live in. Robert Wilson created textless but formally beautiful compositions on stage, giving time a shape as a composer might.

But doesn't the essence of theatre really lie not in its aesthetic possibilities but instead in its special ability to reflect the real world, its special ability to serve as a mirror? Is theatre not a way of putting a frame around a picture of society, so that we may observe the operation of social forces and of the individual psychology that lies beneath them? Should theatre not be principally an attempt to search for truth?

Alternatively, one might emphasize the capacity of theatre to provide a forum, a gathering place, where society can meet and discuss its own future, its problems, and its needs. Or some might emphasize the fact that theatre is unique in its ability not merely to present ideas but to show at the same time the environment and the human situations from which those ideas spring.

But finally, though, there are many who would say that theatre really, in its essence, is a form of diversion, like striptease, clowning, or a carnival freak show, whose central goal must be to entertain.

Should a playwright be compared to a pastry chef in an expensive restaurant—one of those whose role it is to lighten the burden of an elite class by serving it agreeable and evanescent miniature delights? Or to a prostitute who soothes and comforts a client according to the client's specific desires? Is a playwright like an orator in the marketplace rousing people to action, or a preacher offering a sermon in church, or a friend who speaks at a dinner table?

And then there's the question: Can a play in a theatre intervene in the life of a person in the audience?

As I began to write my first plays, I could easily sense that, at least in my country, there were no generally shared beliefs about the purpose of theatre. The audiences, the critics, the playwrights, the actors, had reached no conclusions. One could clearly see that they gathered, they assembled, and plays were put on, but no one had decided what the plays were for.

By way of comparison, one could look at the field of music and observe a somewhat different situation. The goal and intention of certain musical performances could, for example, actually be discerned, relatively speaking, and critical judgments therefore were, relatively speaking, possible to make. People could give their views, for example, on all sorts of singers in all sorts of categories—on classical singers and folk singers, rock singers and jazz singers—and a degree of consensus could even be reached, because critics and audiences shared with the artists an understanding of what some of the criteria were in each category. Within the different categories, different rules were applied, because each one was aiming at something different, and this was a situation that caused no confusion. Everyone knew that Elly Ameling couldn't do what Billie Holiday did, but the point was, she could do something else. And everyone knew where the boundaries were. It was understood that a rock singer might scream, because it was appropriate to rock, while a folk singer might strive for a purity of tone that would be inappropriate to opera or to jazz. Particular music lovers might perhaps have been interested only in opera, but they wouldn't have ridiculed Billie Holiday.

People did not go to concert halls to hear something called "singing." The fact that human beings have the need to hear different sorts of singing, that the appetite for opera cannot be satisfied at a concert of folk music, was recognized in the musical world by the invention of categories. Different sorts of singing even took place in different buildings, with different critics in attendance. But in theatre, obviously, and most particularly in my country, there were no generally accepted categories of plays, there were only "plays." People still had different sorts of appetites for plays, but they didn't know how to find what they wanted. There was a high frustration level and no way to remedy it, as if restaurants had been forbidden by law from announcing the type of food they served, and spaghetti-seekers had no choice but to try every restaurant in town until they hit on one with an Italian chef. And so there was a kind of critical chaos or critical vacuum. Individual audience members and individual critics each expressed and asserted their individual drives and feelings, their incoherent longings, as they made their way from play to play, and what resulted was like a bizarre sort of *imitation* of criticism, in which any criteria at all could be applied to any play at all—a "dream play" in the tradition of Strindberg could be angrily denounced because it lacked the qualities of a Broadway musical, or Thornton Wilder could be excoriated because he didn't write like Eugene O'Neill—and so no sort of consensus could ever be reached on anything, each "opinion" was canceled out by another, and no opinion could be taken seriously.

And that all felt rather agreeable to me, because it meant that no one in theatre would be held to account; if a person wrote a play, as opposed to a poem, for example, there was not going to be any way to prove, or even plausibly to argue, that what he wrote was not good, that what he wrote was in fact a "mistake." It was a field in which one might be left alone, and I leapt into it.

(Of course, if you're actually interested to know all this, you can imagine that it was all, naturally, an unconscious process, and as is probably always the case with choices like this, my decision to get involved with "theatre" was heavily overdetermined, and among the factors were all the usual ones—inclinations, experiences, schools, teachers, for all I know genetic predispositions. From the inside it all felt simply like a matter of instinct: I'd always loved seeing plays and, as a boy, putting on shows of different kinds; when I was twenty-four, I wrote my first full-length, grown-up play, I didn't know why; I found it very exciting, and I never stopped.)

And of course it all turned out to be awfully silly in a way, as one might have predicted. The plays I wrote were, after a few years, actually performed, and I felt very fortunate; but, to my surprise, whenever I ventured out to see one of my own plays, I was always seized by the very strong suspicion that three quarters of the audience were actually sitting there under some awful misapprehension, wondering when the bears on bicycles were going to appear. And they never appeared, and so it was all rather painful and depressing for everybody. In the rather bluntly named little universe of "non-profit" theatre in which I dwelled, people would sign up at different theatres a year in advance to see a "season" of plays, and then they would sign up year after year, and so it seemed to be always the same sad individuals wandering into my plays, again and again, hoping, hoping, hoping for something, then gradually falling into a familiar disappointment, their sadness growing heavier moment by moment, before it all somehow ended and they miserably walked away…I wasn't a sadist, so I didn't enjoy this. And what kind of people, I'd wonder, would insist on going through something like that, night after night? Decades passed, and there they still were. The theatre-goers.

I had decided I wanted to write for the theatre, and that meant that the people who would ultimately hear what I had to say were the theatre-goers. And who were the theatre-goers? In my country they were a small group, altogether, because theatre in the United States has simply never caught on in the way it has in England or on the European continent, for example. Those enormous respectable crowds had never gathered in the United States, the way they had in so many European cities, to watch the plays of Ibsen or Racine. The habit simply had never been formed. For most people in the United States, the issue of theatre just didn't arise. And as for those who, somehow, *had* gone so far as to see a play or two—well, the experience had left most of them rather nonplussed. Having been exposed extensively to the rival storytelling mediums of television and film, most of my fellow-countrymen found it frankly rather peculiar to pay *extra* money to attend an event in which the faces of the actors could barely be seen, and where you had to strain to hear what on earth they were saying (despite the fact that they never stopped shouting, even when standing right next to each other). Theatre obviously was *embarrassing*. It was embarrassing from the first moment, because the actors were trying so hard to fool you, but you never were fooled. You never believed what they seemed to be begging you to believe. Despite the heavy frock coats and the funny hats under which you imagined them sweating, despite the recorded sounds of horses' hooves, sleighbells, and the cracking of the whip, when the actors walked off the stage, you never believed they were going to Kharkhov.

So the theatre-goers in the United States—the loyal followers of theatre, the ones who, despite everything, loved the theatre—the theatre-goers were an odd little circle, a funny old group. Not the sophisticates, one would have to say. Not people who listened to Hugo Wolf or George Crumb or Charlie Parker on their evenings off from the theatre. Not the aesthetes, with their well-worn copies of Kawabata and George Herbert. And, of course, not anyone who was poor or desperate or hungry or oppressed, because theatre is only for the middle class. (People frequently insist, and I suppose I believe it, that in their own times the plays of Shakespeare and Sophocles were part of the life of rich and poor alike, but times have changed, and we have to say that theatre today is very definitely not for everyone. Music is for everyone. Everyone, from the richest of the rich to the poorest of the poor, listens to music. But theatre is only for the middle class.) And in a way these sad wanderers, the lovers of theatre, doggedly attached to a form from the past, for all sorts of reasons unable to take pleasure in the loud, glittering forms of the present, were "my people," to use that phrase that nationalists and tribalists sometimes employ—they were "my people" in that I too loved to sit in a theatre and watch actors act, to follow the story, to listen to the dialogue; I too loved the darkened auditorium, the moment of ecstasy before the play begins; I adored it all, every bit of it. I shared with the group an addiction, a taste, a fetish, a need. It was only in the matter of our preferred "content" that we sometimes parted company. Because I was only mildly drawn to the prewar archetype of bourgeois theatre—elegant aristocrats winking at each other in evening dress—and even less fascinated by the postwar type— animalistic louts roaring and bellowing like wounded beasts. Those worlds on stage didn't really interest me that much. I mean, the aristocrats or the louts would have interested me a lot in real life, or, if I'd seen a documentary about them, I would have been utterly engrossed. It was the fantasies that didn't mean very much to me. They were not my fantasies.

I was in a world—theatre—that was not quite my world. And so as I embarked on a life of writing for the theatre, I felt I was writing, in a way, for no one, because I couldn't help feeling that what I cared about, what I thought about, what I read about, and even the artistic works that were important to me, would all quite possibly be of very little interest to most of the people who would be coming to see my plays.

Now, if you write with the expectation that what you say will be heard and understood, then you and your audience are actually involved in a common endeavor, and while you're writing, they're sitting there beside you, helping you to know how best to reach them. And this help is a wonderful thing. If you're writing to "make your living" as well, a further valuable discipline asserts itself, because the more successful you are in speaking to your audience directly and clearly, the nicer the life you'll be able to lead. This is called the discipline of the market, and it can indeed drive people to accomplish things they couldn't have accomplished without it.

Well, I didn't expect to be understood, and I quickly realized that I'd never be able to "make my living" as a writer of plays (assuming as I did, without ever thinking about it, that my "living" obviously had to include at least the minimum of bourgeois amenities—telephones, heating, "good food," etc.).

Clearly it was an odd position. There was a certain ghostliness, one might very well say, about writing for people who probably wouldn't be interested. And that sense of a flat landscape stretching out forever was heightened by the fact that, as a writer for the theatre, I was not joining an artistic community committed to any particular struggle or agenda. The cafés of the Impressionists and the bars of the Abstract Expressionists had no equivalents on the streets I traveled. I didn't live in a world like Renaissance Florence, in which sculptors vied for the honor of putting their particular subtly different vision of a hero or a god in a public square, because as far as I could see there were no types or models toward which I ought to strive, no public squares, and, in a way, no public.

No one would reward me, and no one would punish me, if I followed the conventions of nineteenth-century theatre or rejected them, if I wrote in a more naturalistic style or in a more surrealistic style. In writing a play, should I draw my inspiration from George Balanchine's ballets? Frederick Wiseman's documentaries? The verses of James Merrill, Fra Angelico's frescoes, the songs on the radio, the day's newspaper, my own life? No one cared.

In the corner of the universe where I'd be writing, there'd been a breakdown in the system of rewards and punishments that behaviorists would consider the only possible system for teaching a dog or a writer how to do a task well. And yet the breakdown meant I was totally free.

Well then, what was the outcome? Was the game lost or won? Were the plays worthwhile and valuable, or weren't they? Regrettably, I may never know. Freedom and self-confidence enabled me to write ambitious plays. I amused myself, and then I died, I suppose, with the results of the experiment still undetermined.

TWELVE

READING PLAYS

1997

On the one hand, there's something rather strange about the idea of reading plays. You could certainly say that what a play is, really, is what actors do together in front of an audience—or a one-person play is what one actor does alone in front of an audience. When you see a play, you see people, members of your own species, engaged in their ordinary physical life in front of you—walking, sitting, digesting, growing older, talking to each other, perhaps touching each other. Their names, in the play, are not their "real" names, maybe, and the words they say to each other may previously have been "written"—but a play is basically a physical experience, for the actors and for you, and most of what you're seeing is exactly what you seem to be seeing—the actors *are* talking, they *are* touching, they're thinking, they're feeling things, they're living in front of you a certain portion of their lives that will never come again. The previously written dialogue drives the actors to experiment with saying what is *not* true. The dialogue forces the actor to practice the human skill of lying. And actors do perfect that skill and can become extraordinarily convincing. Sometimes the actors conspire together to fool the audience with lies that everyone knows are lies. One actor says to another, "I just swallowed poison," and that is a lie, and both of them know it, although you in the audience are in some sense fooled. But part of the fascination of theatre comes from the fact that the actors are not always lying. Sometimes one actor may say to another, "I hate you! I hate you!" and the other actor wonders if it might be true, or believes it *is,* while the actor who says it may be secretly thinking, as we do in life, "Could this possibly be what I really mean?" Our daily pretense that we know who we are is abandoned by the actors, who are led by the dialogue to try out the possibility that what they think and feel is not limited by prior decisions about "who they are" or the supposed outlines of their supposed biographies. The dialogue leads the actor who, in daily life, is known as "sensitive" to become, for a while, insensitive instead, while the actor whose acquaintances call him cold becomes warm and compassionate. The dialogue of a play is part of an elaborate network of personal events in the lives of the actors, just as our own dialogue is in our own daily lives.

It is strange, then, to isolate the dialogue of a play in a book, and it's strange to read it—to sit somewhere alone and read it silently to yourself. Reading a recipe is not the same as eating a cake. Reading about love-making is not the same as making love.

And yet, on the other hand, one has to say that a written play can have a special magic of its own. Reading a recipe may only remind you of the cake that you wish you could have in front of you, but reading a play can be a rather complete experience. The written play has its own music, its own very pristine existence—words, thoughts, and spirit abstracted from the physical, abstracted from the bodies of actors and their travails through space. There are wonderful things that can happen in the mind of a reader that cannot happen to anyone watching actors in a play. Indeed, the actors are often aspiring, as they act, to approach, in physical reality, the experience they had originally when they themselves read the play—but, as the reading experience is in an entirely different realm, they can never quite manage to hit that target (just as writers may often, with an equal degree of un-success—for the very same reason—attempt to capture in words a powerful mood or a feeling that overwhelmed them in life).

More and more I've come to think (perhaps you'll find this self-serving) that to call plays or stories or poems "good" or "bad" is often not very illuminating, whereas it can at times be extremely helpful to notice that "right now, when I read these particular poems, I feel well, I feel happy, I feel that I am getting something that I have needed." It's not that those poems are "the best" poems or that they're "better" than certain others, but that for you, now, they are important and right. Animals in the forest require certain nutrients, and they learn how to find them. They don't all need the same things, and they don't need the same things at every stage in their lives. The nuts that a particular badger finds of very little value may turn out to be crucial for a particular squirrel. As writers, we can't predict who might come along who might find our offerings valuable. But because we've all been readers, we know what the experience is like, and we hope that what certain writers have given to us, we will give to someone.

THIRTEEN

AESTHETIC PREFERENCES

2008

It's easier to sleep if your head is elevated, and so people use pillows. If you want to attach one piece of cloth to another piece of cloth, a sewing machine can be extremely helpful, and that's why Isaac M. Singer made sewing machines. But why do people make and use what we call "artistic" objects?

It's a question that seems particularly puzzling if you make such objects yourself, in a way devoting your life to it, without quite knowing why you're doing it.

George Gershwin might possibly have wondered to himself, "Why do I write songs?" and yet, as soon as he wrote them, many, many of his fellow humans were eager to sing them, and others were dying to listen to them, and when they heard them, they all felt better and happier. So even though, in a way, those facts don't quite answer the original question—they don't quite explain Gershwin's drive to write music—still, in another way, what more of an answer could Gershwin possibly have wanted?

Everyone knows that if you're hungry and depressed, a little ice cream can bring a moment of relief, and that's why we like it.

I presented my early plays to the world with many of the same feelings that Gershwin probably felt when he presented his songs—in each case I had given my all and done my best to make something that I found pleasing.

Nonetheless, my first professional production in New York (in 1975) provoked a level of hostility in its small audience that was seriously disturbing. In my second production, the anger of the audience seemed to diminish a bit, but they seemed stricken and miserable instead—hurt, or baffled.

Every day I wake up wondering what has happened to those early plays of mine in the intervening years. They haven't caught on, apparently, even after all this time. And the years I spent writing them—what were those years? Were they like the years that recovered alcoholics describe—"lost years" spent wandering in a desperate haze from one night's incomprehensible encounter with someone or other to the next night's horrible barroom brawl?

Not long ago, I made a film with a group of people, and we'd poured a significant portion of our lives into making it, along with quite a bit of thought and passion, and finally it was shown at a film festival. And when the screening of the film was over, a moderator asked the audience if anyone had any questions for the filmmakers. Almost instantly, a man spoke up from the center of the auditorium. "Yes, I have a question," he said in a loud voice. "What was the point of that?" Now, let's note that his question could have meant two different things. He might have been wondering what the point was for us in making the film. Or he might have been asking what point there could possibly have been for him in watching it. But in a way, I feel that my whole life seems to revolve around the fact that I'm crawling through the streets every day unable to answer either version of that question about anything I do.

You have to understand, I do read my plays myself every few years, including the ones that people have liked least. I read them, I change a few words, I improve a few lines, and I'm surprised once again that so few people liked them. "What *is* it about me and all those other people?" I think to myself. I like orange juice, and so do they. I like the performances of Roseanne Barr and Robert De Niro, and so do they. But I like my own plays, and they don't. Why is that?

People always say that "tastes differ," and that that's just a fact. A lot of people like spinach. Many fewer like dandelion greens. When certain people take their clothes off in public, they're worshipped and rewarded, while others are arrested or taken to an insane asylum. But if you have a stake in the answer, it's hard not to ask, "Why the spinach? Why not the greens?" Is there no comprehensible reason that the spinach is more popular?

Of course there *are* answers, but you'd have to devote your life to a scientific study of preferences in vegetables in order to begin to find out about preferences in vegetables, and it would be the same with all other areas of preference.

Leaving aside my own plays, I've always been curious why, in comparison to most people I know, I enjoy plays in general so much. I can't, obviously, answer that question either.

I do like plays, though. There's something so chaotic about them. And I like to write the text that appears in a play, that is part of a play. For me, a play is a wonderful pile-up of bodies, lights, sets, gestures, clothes, nudity, music, dance, and running through it all and driving it all is a stream of words, sentences. Words and sentences are (to me) aesthetic materials, and a purpose that I think one would have to call aesthetic can certainly be the governing element in writing a play. One plays with sentences the way a child plays with matches—because they're unpredictable. In fact, sentences make up a sort of jungle in which I seem to be living. And somehow an artistic object comes into being, that is, an object that exists for the purpose of being contemplated.

And the contemplation of an artistic object can induce a sort of daytime dream, one might say. And perhaps it's somewhat odd for a play to have that intention, at least in comparison to a painting, for example. Agnes Martin's paintings put the viewer into a trance, while Bertolt Brecht's plays were specifically designed to wake people up. But a play might possibly try to do both.

I wonder if the daytime dreams induced by artistic objects may not be really rather necessary for people, as nighttime dreams unquestionably are. If they weren't necessary, then why would every culture on earth invent music, songs, poetry, what have you? Perhaps it's the case that, in order to live, we must process our experience first rationally, and then irrationally. But if such dreams are actually necessary in fact, that goes some way to explaining the horrible atmosphere that has hovered in various rooms in which my plays have been performed. In other words, at night we can all create for ourselves the dreams that we need, but the creation of the artistic objects that stimulate our daytime dreams is contracted out to a particular group of people, and in our society it's a self-appointed group. So naturally the various dreams that we dream at night are not criticized by anybody—there are no reviewers in the Land of Nod—nor do we need to defend our dreams or make any claims for them. But as we all find ourselves in the frustrating situation that most of the artistic objects we need and depend on for our daytime dreams must be made by other people, it's not surprising that we're finicky, critical and sometimes even angry when these objects are presented to us—we're constantly complaining, like diners in a restaurant who repeatedly send bad-tasting dishes back to the kitchen. And then, perhaps inevitably, centuries ago, analysts of art brought the concepts of "good" and "bad" into the conversation, and most of us, as irritable diners, frequently use this vocabulary in discussing our artistic meals, although it often merely adds to the prevailing confusion, because a parsnip is not really a "bad" carrot, it's a different vegetable.

So. What type of dreams do you enjoy? There are clearly different categories of dreams that vie for primacy in each human soul.

Some are dreams of conquest, victory, or revenge. Others are dreams of sensuality, beauty, joy, kindness, and love. Artistic objects are not brainwashing machines. They have influence, not power. But I think we're influenced by our daytime dreams, just as much as we're influenced by our family and friends and our personal experiences. So to me it's reasonable to think that a world in which Chuang Tzu and George Eliot are widely read will be less dangerous than a world in which people read only sadistic stories or military magazines.

Certain theorists definitely disagree with that opinion. Actually, there are people who dwell almost obsessively on the fact that an exposure to "art" did not prevent certain famous men from doing horrible things. I feel I've been frequently reminded, for example, that the Nazi leader Reinhard Heydrich played Mozart on the violin during the same period in which he planned the extermination of the Jews. But my speculation on this, if I may offer one, is that, perhaps because of his history and who he was, Commander Heydrich did not fully absorb the human possibilities that others have grasped through listening to the music of Mozart. Similarly, the young English major Seung-Hui Cho killed thirty-two people in a famous massacre at a college in Virginia, even though a kindly professor of English had given him private tutorials in creative writing and had even tried to speak to him sympathetically about his own problems. She did her best, but Cho was too deeply trapped in the quicksand of his own mind, and the lessons in creative writing didn't save him. He didn't hear enough, or understand enough, of what his teacher was trying to tell him. Mozart, being a composer of music rather than a supernatural creature from outer space, was not up to the task of convincing Reinhard Heydrich to get off the path he was on and move to another one. But just as the failure of Cho's teacher can hardly lead us to say that no kindly teacher has ever helped or saved a student, so it seems preposterous to leap from Mozart's inability to reconstruct Reinhard Heydrich to the claim that composers, painters, and writers have not influenced the world by offering humanity their wisdom and their vision of what life could be.

Dreams can help, although they don't make their points in a direct way, and sometimes no one can say for sure exactly what their points really are. Dreams can even agitate for change, or for a better world, sometimes simply by offering people a glimpse of something agreeable that might be pursued—or crystallizing into a vivid nightmare something awful that ought to be avoided. Dreams are actually involved in a serious battle. Despite a certain lightness in their presentation, they're not joking.

FOURTEEN

INTERVIEW WITH MARK STRAND

1998

The American poet Mark Strand says that the elements he requires in order to be able to write are "a place, a desk, a familiar room. I need some of my books there. I need quiet. That's about it." Asked if he ever writes in a less tranquil spot, such as on a train, he replies that he does, but usually only prose, because it's "less embarrassing. Who would understand a man of my age writing reams of poetry on a train, if they looked over my shoulder? I would be perceived as an overly emotional person."

Wallace Shawn: I started reading that thing that that guy wrote about you. But it upset me, because he kept talking about the themes of your writing, and I didn't get it. I don't think I really get the concept of "themes." So I'm not going to ask you questions like, What is your view of nothingness? because I don't get that, exactly.

Mark Strand: I don't get it either. And I'm not sure I could articulate a view of nothingness, since nothingness doesn't allow a description of itself. Once you start describing nothingness, you end up with somethingness.

WS: In any case, do we read poetry because we're interested in "themes"?

MS: You don't read poetry for the kind of truth that passes for truth in the workaday world. You don't read a poem to find out how to get to Twenty-fourth Street. You don't read a poem to find the meaning of life. The opposite. I mean, you'd be foolish to. Now, some American poets present the reader with a slice of life, saying, "I went to the store today, and I saw a man, and he looked at me, and I looked at him, and we both knew we were…thieves. And aren't we all thieves?" You know, this is extracting from everyday experience a statement about life, or a moral. But there is another type of poetry, in which the poet provides the reader with a surrogate world through which he reads *this* world. Wallace Stevens was the twentieth-century master of this. There's no other poetry that *sounds* like a Wallace Stevens poem. But then, there's nothing that sounds like a Frost poem, either. Or a Hardy poem. These people have created worlds of their own. Their language is so forceful and identifiable that you read them not to verify the meaning or truthfulness of your own experience of the world, but simply because you want to saturate yourself with their particular voices.

WS: Well, your poetry is obviously very much in this category. When we read your poetry, we are enticed by the voice—and then led into a world that you have created. And at first, I would say, we can more or less picture or imagine the scenes you conjure up, although they may consist of elements that in our daily world would never be combined in the way you've combined them. Sometimes, though, in your poems—quite often, really—we reach a point that is almost, one could say, Zeno-like, in which we're asked to imagine things that are either almost self-contradictory or literally unimaginable. I mean, in a surrealist painting, a painter could present a very strange landscape, but he couldn't present one like this! This couldn't be painted!

MS: Well, I think what happens at certain points in my poems is that language takes over, and I follow it. It just sounds right. And I trust the implication of what I'm saying, even though I'm not absolutely sure what it is that I'm saying. I'm just willing to let it be. Because if I were absolutely sure of whatever it was that I said in my poems, if I were sure, and could verify it and check it out and feel, yes, I've said what I intended, I don't think the poem would be smarter than I am. I think the poem would be, finally, a reducible item. It's this "beyondness," that depth that you reach in a poem, that keeps you returning to it. And you wonder—the poem seemed so natural at the beginning—how did you get where you ended up? What happened? I mean, I like that, I like it in other people's poems when it happens. I like to be mystified. Because it's really that place which is unreachable, or mysterious, at which the poem becomes ours, finally, becomes the possession of the reader. I mean, in the act of figuring it out, of pursuing meaning, the reader is absorbing the poem, even though there's an *absence* in the poem. But he just has to live with that. And eventually, it becomes essential that it exists in the poem, so that something beyond his understanding, or beyond his experience, or something that doesn't quite match up with his experience, becomes more and more his. He comes into possession of a mystery, you know—which is something that we don't allow ourselves in our lives.

WS: We don't?

MS: I mean, we live with mystery, but we don't like the feeling. I think we should get used to it. We feel we have to know what things mean, to be on top of this and that. I don't think it's human, you know, to be that competent at life. That attitude is far from poetry.

WS: An experience of total immersion in mystery that I once had was reading the first half of Heidegger's *Being and Time*. You know, it was really totally up to you to sort of create this world in your own head, and whether what was in your head was what was in Heidegger's head—who could possibly guess?

MS: Well, when I read poetry I can't imagine that what's in the reader's head is ever what was in the poet's head, because there's usually very little in the poet's head.

WS: You mean...

MS: I mean, I think the reality of the poem is a very ghostly one. It doesn't try for the kind of concreteness that fiction tries for. It doesn't ask you to imagine a place in detail; it suggests, it suggests, it suggests again. I mean, as *I* write it. William Carlos Williams had other ideas.

WS: But do you suggest something that you yourself have already pictured?

MS: I'm picturing it as I'm writing it. I'm putting together what I need in order to have this thing be alive. But sometimes it's more complete than at other times.

WS: When you say that when you write, language takes over, and then you follow it, you're implying that the experience of writing is one in which, at least to some extent, you're in a passive role. Something is coming to you from somewhere, and you're receiving it. But where is it coming from? Is it *just* the unconscious?

MS: Poems aren't dreams. They just aren't. It's something else. People who write down their dreams and think they're poems are wrong. They're neither dreams nor poems.

WS: But the type of poetry you're describing can be frustrating to the reader. A lot of people I know would have to admit that their basic model for what reading is would be something like the experience of reading the newspaper. Each sentence is supposed to match up to a particular slice of reality.

MS: If you want a poem to say what it means, right away, clearly—well, what happens when you read that kind of poem is that it puts you back in the world that you know. The poem makes that world seem a little more comfortable, because here is somebody else who has had an experience like yours. But you see, these little anecdotes that we read in these poems and that we like to believe are true, are in fact fictions. They represent a reduction of the real world. There's so much in our experience that we take for granted— we don't need to read poems that help us to take those things even *more* for granted. People like John Ashbery or Stevens do just the opposite—they try to explode those reductions. There's a desire in Ashbery, for example, to create perfect non sequiturs, to continually take us off guard. He creates a world that is fractured. But, looking at it from another point of view, you *could* say that it's simply a world that is as fractured and as unpredictable as the world in which we move every day. So there's an element of delight in these people who rearrange reality. We usually hang on to the predictability of our experiences to such an extent…and there's nowhere else where one can escape that as thoroughly as one can in certain poets' work. When I read poetry, I want to feel myself suddenly larger…in touch with—or at least close to—what I deem magical, astonishing. I want to experience a kind of wonderment. And when you report back to your own daily world after experiencing the strangeness of a world sort of recombined and reordered in the depths of a poet's soul, the world looks fresher somehow. Your daily world has been taken out of context. It has the voice of the poet written all over it, for one thing, but it also seems suddenly more alive—not as routinely there.

WS: Of course, when you talk about poetry in that way, you're going on the assumption that your reader is willing to put quite a bit of effort into following you—in contrast to writing for the theatre, for example, where it's more normal for one's colleagues to say, "The people aren't going to get this. Clarify it."

MS: I think a poet writes a poem not feeling that he must be understood on the first or second reading. He writes a poem hoping that the poem will be read more than once or twice, and its meaning will be revealed over the course of time, or its meaning will reveal itself over the course of time.

WS: When you say you hope that a poem will be read more than once or twice, how many times do you mean? How many times do *you* read a poem?

MS: When I write my own poems, I read them hundreds of times to myself. But when I read other people's poems I will read them dozens of times, sometimes more than dozens of times. I don't know why this should seem strange. The average churchgoing person who lives in the Bible Belt will have read the same passages in the Bible hundreds of times, and they will have revealed to him more each time.

WS: An actor in a play goes through a similar process, really, and acting could in a sense be seen as a form of reading, I suppose. The actor goes over the text hundreds of times, seeing more and more implications and different possible meanings inside each individual line, and at the same time seeing through the various clichés of interpretation with which he has at first mistakenly overlaid each line.

MS: Well, a good reader of poetry may be very much like an actor working on his part, because he reads the poem aloud to himself again and again, and sometimes he learns it by heart. And it becomes familiar. It, finally, becomes part of him. A poem releases itself, secretes itself, slowly—almost, sometimes, poisonously—into the mind of the reader. It does it with cadence, it does it with combinations that might strike the reader as beautiful. Of course, God knows what the beautiful is. I don't know. Because the beautiful fifty years from now will be what is seen as the ugly now or what's insupportable now or barely tolerated now. But, you know, I think if you try too hard to be immediately comprehensible to your audience, if you give too much to the moment, you're also giving too much to the status quo. The poet's obligation isn't to his audience, primarily, but to the language that he hopes he's perpetuating. And when you think of how long it takes us to understand each other, for example—and how much leeway we give other areas of knowledge in our lives—why can't we be a little more patient with poetry? The language of a poem is meant to be meditated on. You clear a psychic space for poetry. It's a space in which words loom large.

WS: But how does a person prepare such a psychic space?

MS: Well, if you spend a lot of time alone, particularly if you're thinking about your life, or other people's lives, you're already used to the space I'm talking about. There are certain painters I know to whom the language of poetry means a great deal. And it may be because these people spend a lot of time in front of canvases, alone, with nobody to talk to, that they're prepared: they're ready to take the poem in. Their minds are not full of a lot of noise and clutter and unfulfilled desire. I mean, you have to be willing to *read* poetry; you have to be willing to meet it halfway—because it won't go any further than that if it's any good. A poem has its dignity, after all. I mean, a poem shouldn't beg you to read it; it's pathetic, if that's the case. Some poets fear that they won't be heard unless they flatter the reader, go 90 percent of the way, do it all for the reader. But that's pathetic.

WS: Damn! I'm sort of worried that we're not living in the right world to read what you and the poets you admire are writing.

MS: Well, poetry—at least lyric poetry—tries to lead us to relocate ourselves in the self. But everything we want to do these days is an escape from self. People don't want to sit home and think. They want to sit home and watch television. Or they want to go out and have fun. And having fun is not usually meditative. It doesn't have anything to do with reassessing one's experience and finding out who one is or who the other guy is. It has to do with burning energy. When you go to the movies, you're overcome with special effects and monstrous goings-on. Things unfold with a rapidity that's thrilling. You're not given a second to contemplate the previous scene, to meditate on something that's just happened. Something else takes its place. We forget that there is a thrill that attends the slower pleasures, pleasures that become increasingly powerful the more time we spend pursuing them.

WS: Maybe language in general is slowly losing out in some sort of weird competition in the world.

MS: Well, but on the other hand, we do talk to one another. We would be lonely if we didn't use words.

WS: Maybe people avoid poetry because it somehow actively makes them nervous or anxious.

MS: They don't want to feel the proximity of the unknown—or the mysterious. It's too deathlike; it's too threatening. It suggests the possibility of loss of control right around the corner.

WS: When you say deathlike…

MS: Well, when I say the unknown—death is the great unknown. I mean, most lyric poems lead to some acknowledgment of death. In fact, most poems are dark and dreary affairs that have to do with death and dying, or loss of one sort or another—loss of love, loss of friends, loss of life. Most lyric poems are sad, because if you think deeply at all about your experience, you think about your experience in time—your life—and if you're thinking about your life, you can't avoid the fact that it will end in death. In fact, everything about a poem—the meter of the poem, or the measure of the poem—is a reminder of time. Even a line that's repeated: we're back again. I think that the popularity of villanelles or poems that use refrains, is caused by the fact that they seem to enact a stay against time, they seem to give us a momentary reprieve from what usually is the subject of the poem, or the matter of the poem. So, although the poem may be about dying or death, we have repeated lines that seem to say we haven't really gone anywhere, we're back again. But in the end, that just helps us to hold on to the loss that is in the poem. It helps us to remember it.

WS: In some of your own poems, death is kind of disturbing, but in others, it isn't that bad...But if poetry in a way is inherently disturbing and likely to provoke anxiety, is prose any different?

MS: Well, I think a poet's focus is not quite what a prose writer's is; it's not entirely on the world outside. It's fixed on that area where the inside meets the outside, where the poet's sensibility meets the weather, meets the street, meets other people, meets what he reads. So a poet describes that point of contact: the self, the edge of the self, and the edge of the world. That shadow land between self and reality. Sometimes the focus is tipped slightly in favor of the self, sometimes, more objectively, in favor of the world. And so sometimes, when the balance is tipped toward the self, strange things are said, odd things get into the poem. Because the farther you are from the world that everybody recognizes as the world, the stranger things look. I mean, some novels do this, but most don't. There are some narrators who insert themselves, as Philip Roth does brilliantly and amazingly. I'm always dazzled by his books. The world is electrically alive in *American Pastoral*, for example, but he's there, too: Roth is Zuckerman, and he's there, he's telling the story. In a sense, that book is more magical than any poem I've read recently.

WS: I had no idea you were such a Philip Roth fan. So am I! Do you think of yourself as someone who reads widely in many different sorts of books? Would you call yourself a person who spends a lot of time reading?

MS: I have gone through periods in my life of reading a great deal, and others in which I barely touched a book. There are certain novels I enjoy reading and rereading. There are poets I read and reread. There was a period at one time when I read Wittgenstein. There was a period when I read the romantic poets, and would read Wordsworth quite a lot. There was never a period in my adult life when I didn't read and reread Wallace Stevens, or Elizabeth Bishop. There's never been a period in my adult life when I haven't derived pleasure from reading Philip Roth or, on the other hand, Samuel Beckett. Or Italo Calvino, or Tommaso Landolfi. Or Bruno Schulz, or Franz Kafka. Great poets like Octavio Paz I've read and reread over the years, Joseph Brodsky, Derek Walcott. There are also younger poets I read with a sense of awe: Jorie Graham, Charles Wright, Charles Simic.

WS: What did you mean when you said that a poet's first responsibility was to the language?

MS: Well, in writing poetry, one wants a certain flexibility in the use of language, a flexibility that can keep alive successes in the language from the past, that is, other poems, and that will also ensure that whatever poetry comes next will capitalize on the successes instead of on the failures. The fact is that we take many of our cues on how to proceed, and our ideas about what is a good line, or a beautiful line, from what we've experienced from the poetry of the past. In other words, it would be nice to know that poets in the future will have read the best poets of today and yesterday, that they won't simply base their poems on news reports or instruction manuals. You know, so that there's some continuity in the language of poetry. Because it's complicated, but we're defined by the best that's written in our language, and so we want to perpetuate the best that's written in our language. If poetry becomes just a revision of the newspaper page or the talking heads on TV, that's not a language that will last; it's not a language that translates into the future.

WS: But then what would you think of a poet, or someone who said he was a poet, a student, let's say, who came to you and said, "Well, I'm only interested in the present. I don't know about the poetry of the past, I don't like it, and I'm not too interested in it"?

MS: Well, I would ask him, "What poetry have you read that makes you feel that you want to write poetry?" Because usually what draws us toward poetry is the individual voice that we want to hear—the voice of Wordsworth, the voice of Keats, James Merrill, Anthony Hecht, whoever it is. The chances are that a person who doesn't feel any desire to hear such voices may not turn out to have a very original voice himself.

WS: So you do in a way agree with the academic writers who always seem to imply that the parents of poems are other poems, as opposed to what I'm always wondering, which is why couldn't the greatest influences on a poet be the people he's known, or the experiences he's had every day, rather than the poems he's read?

MS: Well, it all depends on the poetry you write. Some people may be more influenced by their mothers and less influenced by Robert Frost. It differs with different poets. But by and large, I think poets are more influenced by other poems than they are by what they eat and whom they talk to—because they read other poems deeply, and sometimes they don't eat dinner deeply or chat with a friend over the telephone deeply. Because poems not only demand patience, they demand a kind of surrender. You must give yourself up to them. Once you've done that, and allowed them to enter into your system, of course they're going to be more influential. This is the real food for a poet: other poems, not meatloaf.

WS: But what about the idea that a poet should be influenced by a wide range of experience, that a poet should explore *life* and allow it to affect him? Don't you have any feeling that you should do everything, at least once?

MS: I don't have to try everything on the menu to know what it is that I like. I can make a reasonable guess as to what I *might* like, and so that's what I will order. I don't go out of my way to experience every possible thing, because that's dangerous. I want to protect myself. I want not to experience many, many different things, but to experience the things I choose to experience well, and deeply.

WS: Some writers, for example, have tried to enhance their work by writing under the influence of alcohol or drugs.

MS: They interfere. I mean, if I've had a couple of drinks, I don't feel like writing. I feel like having another drink. Or I feel like going to sleep.

WS: But if poems, including poems from the past, are really a poet's main food, doesn't that lead to some rather odd consequences? For example, poets always seem to love to quote other poems in their poetry. I mean—my God—if a contemporary playwright put lines from some nineteenth-century play in one of his own plays, it would be considered, well, ludicrously academic.

MS: Well, too much of that can be burdensome or overbearing. But sometimes it's delightful; sometimes there's a perfect line that just fits in your poem, and it comes from a poem that's a hundred years old. Poetry is always building these connections. It's not showing off. It's the verbalization of the internal life of man. And each poet forges a link in the chain, so that it can go on. That may be a grandiose way to think of it, but it's certainly not academic. I mean, academics really know very little about poetry; they experience it from the outside. Some of them are ideal readers, but their job is to make connections. It's the way they read, the way they have to read. But why should we allow the reading of an academic to become a paradigm for the way we *all* should read?

WS: Well, but some modern poetry, like *The Waste Land*, has been so full of connections—connections and allusions—that emergency academic help has been required in order to read it.

MS: Yes, it would have been impossible for me to have read *The Waste Land* without critical intervention.

WS: But isn't there something wrong with that? Or don't you think so? I mean, you don't write like that.

MS: No.

WS: Well, why don't you? Would you write that way if you felt like it—or do you have any objection to that?

MS: I don't. I mean, Eliot was a very learned guy and, you know—he wrote a very allusive poetry. My poetry is much more self-contained. I think that there are all kinds of poetry possible—

there are all kinds of people possible. *The Waste Land*, the *Cantos* of Pound—this is one kind of poetry. It's a very extreme case of allusiveness. These are men who were intent on revising culture; that found its way into their poetry.

WS: And you're willing to make that journey?

MS: Sure!

WS: It's worth it? You don't think it's an outrageous thing to do?

MS: No. By what standard would it be outrageous? Only by the standard of how easily one can understand the daily newspaper. But say one's standard were trying to understand what is most difficult and most elusive in ourselves. How do we know who we are, and what we are? How do we know why we said what we said? If you use that as a standard, then *The Waste Land* becomes simple. Well, less difficult.

WS: The problem is that, because of the existence of very allusive modern poetry, a lot of people, at least in my generation, were given in their school days a sort of screwy idea of what poetry *is*, and it put them off poetry for life. I'm very grateful that I had some wonderful English teachers, because the bad ones did try to teach us that poetry was simply a game, in which you substituted a certain group of words for the code words offered by the poet. When the poet said *water*, you crossed it out and wrote *rebirth*, et cetera. It was all, "This is a symbol of this, this is a symbol of that." And in a certain way, we got to *hate* those symbols.

MS: Well, rightfully. It sounds tyrannical on the part of the teacher to submit you, and to submit the poem, to that. I mean, I don't think teachers who are forced to teach poetry know why they're teaching it, or what poetry provides. Some poems aren't paraphrasable, just as some experiences can't be readily understood—and yet we live with those experiences. I mean, we can love a poem and not understand it, I think. There's no reason why we can't live with a poem that doesn't deliver meaning right away—or perhaps ever. You know, somebody should have asked the teacher, "What's the relationship between the meaning of a poem and the *experience* of a poem?"

WS: We didn't have an experience!

MS: It's as if the paraphrase of the poem was meant to take the place of the poem, and the poem was lost.

WS: I'm afraid so.

MS: You know, the idea is to experience the poem! But this is the reversal that takes place: the poem becomes a surrogate for what the teacher has to say about it.

WS: Well, I mean, *literally*, because in my old schoolbooks, the physical poem is actually obliterated by the notes I've taken on the teacher's interpretations. The page is a swirl of arrows and circles and scrawled-in words. You could never read the original poem.

MS: I don't know why teachers are afraid of the *experience* of the poem…

WS: Well, because it would be like passing out drugs in class, I imagine.

MS: Poetry *is* a high. It is a thrill. If people were taught to read poetry in the right way, they would find it extremely pleasurable.

WS: It's also an experience of close contact with another mind, another person.

MS: Well, certainly something I would want a reader to have as he experiences my poetry is—a form of intimacy.

WS: Yes. But of course—how can I put this—as a reader, I wouldn't want to have that intimacy with everybody.

MS: No. You have to like the voice. I mean, you have to like the music you hear.

WS: Right. And it's quite a personal and individual matter what voices you like. It's hard to predict. Like a lot of our other most personal preferences, it goes deep into the individual psyche.

MS: Well, I feel that anything is possible in a poem. But the problem is, as a poet develops, he develops a predisposition to use certain words—which create or suggest certain landscapes, or interiors, or certain attitudes. Those, in fact, become his identity as a poet. So when a subject with a vocabulary he has never used asserts itself, it may be difficult to accommodate. It will seem strange and may eventually be repudiated in favor of the words that he or she knows will work, because finally—despite experimentation and all the self-righteousness attendant on experimentation—it's more of our own poems that we want to write, more of *our own poems*, poems that sound like they were written by us. It's a terrible limitation. I mean, in some ways, this is where John Ashbery's genius is so marked— that he's got such a large vocabulary that it accomodates everything. He can talk about Goebbels, or hummingbirds, steam shovels and hemorrhoids, all in the same poem. And he could do it, probably, within ten lines and it would sound like Ashbery!

WS: Allen Ginsberg once implied that he wrote "Howl" in one draft, without revising it, although later he said he actually did revise it a lot. Have you ever been interested in trying the no-revision approach?

MS: Well, I would *like* to write just one draft of a poem and have done with it, but it rarely happens. It's only happened a very few times. You know, I'm not one of the geniuses that gets it right the first time. But there are people who do.

WS: Well, there *may* be. We'll never know—they may secretly be hiding a thousand drafts of their poems. Anyway, who cares? If we read something and we like it, we don't care whether it took someone a long time or a short time to write it.

MS: I don't think the writer should care. We're lucky to write a few terrific things in our lifetime, and for all we know, we may already have written them. So, who knows? I know nothing of the value of my work—all I know is that it's what I do, and what I love to do.

WS: Did you feel differently when you were thirty? Because I did.

MS: Oh, I felt very differently. I was much more ambitious. I felt that I was destined to hold a special place. That's what I needed in those days to keep me writing. I don't need that anymore, and I don't believe any of that obtains. But if young writers talk to me in those terms, I understand very well what they mean, and I'm sympathetic.

WS: But all the same, doesn't it sometimes bother you that millions of people don't revere you? I mean, don't you sometimes feel that you ought to be honored for your accomplishments everywhere you go? After all, you *deserve* it.

MS: Well, some people like my poetry a great deal. It's better than *nobody* liking it.

WS: But what about the millions of other people?

MS: There are a few people I know whose feeling about my poetry is the most important thing to me. It's as simple as that. I don't know many of the people who read my poems. I don't even know, when they read my poems, whether they like my poems. There's no way for me to know, so I can't worry about it.

WS: Yes, but all the same, don't you sometimes resent the fact that certain other people in our culture are so incredibly idolized? For example, I was recently listening to a CD of Elliott Carter, and I was thinking, Isn't it unbelievable that this man, who has created such incredibly subtle and beautiful music, is much less honored in our society than people who write songs using only three or four chords? Doesn't he have a reason to be outraged about that?

MS: Well, the people who like those three or four chords probably aren't going to like his music.

WS: No.

MS: And he probably wouldn't want to be popular with that set.

MS: No, he wouldn't.

MS: So there's no complaint.

WS: You mean, these are two different audiences. So that would be like playing elephant music to giraffes.

MS: There is only one reason to be envious of the people who write very successful songs with three or four chords, and that is that they earn the kind of money that gives them a kind of freedom that Elliott Carter may not have. So it would be nice for Elliott Carter to go to the restaurants that Elton John can afford. But if the price was that he had to write music exactly like Elton John's, then he would do without it. And that's it. If I had to write the kind of sentences that Jacqueline Susann wrote, you know, write the kind of novels that she wrote, I wouldn't be able to hold my head high anywhere! I'd *slink* into restaurants—very expensive restaurants—and I'd *slink* into expensive hotels. And I'd be ashamed to say what it was that I did.

WS: But don't you find it sort of awful that our society doesn't even respect poetry enough to allow poets to support themselves through their writing?

MS: I think poetry would be different if people could make a living writing poetry. Then you would have to satisfy certain expectations. Instead of the inherited norms by which we recognize poems to be poems, there would be a whole new set of constraints, and not such enduring ones, having to do with the marketplace, having to do with what sells, or what engages people in the short run. So perhaps poetry is better off having no monetary value.

WS: If I may speak of you personally, it seems that, for better or worse, writing poetry is an essential part of your identity, your sense of yourself—am I right about that?

MS: Well, my identity is hopelessly wrapped up in what I write, and my being a writer. If I stopped writing, I would simply feel the loss of myself. When I don't write, I don't feel properly alive. There was a period in my life, for five years, when I didn't write any poems. They were among the saddest years of my life, perhaps the saddest years. I wrote a lot of other things. None of them satisfied me the way the writing of poetry does, but I did them, just because I had to be ready, in case poetry came back into my life and I felt capable enough to write poems that weren't terrible. I refuse to write if I feel the poems I'm writing are bad. My identity is not that important, finally. Not dishonoring what I consider a noble craft is more impor-

tant. I would rather not write than write badly and dishonor poetry—even if it meant I wasn't properly myself. I mean, this sounds
high and noble, but in fact, it's not. I love poetry. I love myself, but I
think I love poetry as much as I love myself.

WS: You don't seem to share the attitude that some people have
of, "Hey, I enjoy my hedonistic life of reading and writing, and I
don't have the faintest idea whether what I do benefits society or
not, and I couldn't care less."

MS: No. That's not my thing at all. I'm *certain* that what I do,
and what other poets do, is important.

WS: I have to ask you one more personal question. Well, I don't
have to, but I will, because I'm curious: Do you care whether you're
read after you're dead?

MS: Well, not to be funny about this, but I'm sort of split on
the issue. I mean, I would like to be read after I'm dead, but that's
projection.

WS: You mean, because you're imagining…?

MS: I mean, I'd really like to be *alive* after I'm dead. That's all
that is. I don't really think it will make much difference to me when
I'm dead whether I'm read or not.

WS: Right.

MS: Just as whether I'm *dead* or not won't mean much to me when I'm dead. You see?

WS: Sure. So the issue of whether your work is read after your death…

MS: I think most people who have published books, whose career is a matter of public record, will be read for a little while and then dropped. I mean, after a while, almost everybody is dropped to make room for the new. I think that's only fair. I just hope that the new, or the next, includes poetry. That's what I want. Poetry must continue.

FIFTEEN

WRITING ABOUT SEX

2008

For whatever reason, and I don't remember how it happened, I am now what people call "sixty-four years old," and I have to admit that I started writing about sex almost as soon as I realized that it was possible to do so—say, at the age of fourteen—and I still do it, even though I was in a way the wrong age then, and in a different way I guess I'm the wrong age now. Various people who have liked me or cared about me—people who have believed in my promise as a writer—have hinted to me at different times in my life that an excessive preoccupation with the subject of sex has harmed or even ruined my writing. They've implied that it was sad, almost pitiful, that an adolescent obsession—or maybe it was in fact a psychological compulsion—should have been allowed to marginalize what they optimistically had hoped might have been a serious body of work. Meanwhile, people I don't know very well have tended over all those decades to break into a very particular smile, one I recognize now, when they've learned that I've written something that deals with sex—a winking smile that seems to suggest that a trivial, silly, but rather amusing topic has been mentioned. It's a smile not unlike the smile that would appear on the faces of some of our more conservative teachers in the 1950s when the topic of "jazz" was raised—a smile sometimes accompanied back in those gloomy days by a mocking, suggestive swaying of the hips.

I suppose it goes without saying that James Joyce, D. H. Lawrence and others were expanding the scope of literature and redrawing humanity's picture of itself when they approached this subject in the earlier part of the twentieth century. But by the time I came along, many of my friends were embarrassed on my behalf precisely because the topic I was writing about seemed so closely associated with an earlier era.

So why have I stuck with it? I suppose it has to do with the point I've heard boringly expressed by writers in one way or another all of my life—the thing they always say, while in a way always hoping that no one will believe them, though what they're saying is true—some variation or another of "I don't do my own writing." I personally sometimes express the point, when pressed, by saying that I see my writing as a sort of collaboration between my rational self ("me") and the voice that comes from outside the window, the voice that comes in through the window, whose words I write down in a state of weirded-out puzzlement, thinking, "Jesus Christ, what is he saying?"

The collaboration is really quite an unequal partnership, I'd have to admit. The voice contributes everything, and I contribute nothing, frankly, except some modest organizing abilities and (if I may say so) a certain skill in finding, among the voice's many utterances, those that are most interesting. (I suppose I'm quite a bit like one of those young college graduates in jacket and tie who helps some unruly but for some reason celebrated man to write his autobiography.) When I try to define the voice, I say, weakly, "Oh, that's the unconscious," but I'm eventually forced to conclude that, if the unconscious has thoughts, it has to have heard these thoughts (or at least their constituent fragments) from human beings of some description—from the people I've met, the people I've read about, the people I've happened to overhear on the street. So it's not just a theory that society is speaking to itself through me. If it were not so, all I would be able to hear, and all I would be trying to transcribe, would be the sound of my own heart sending blood through my veins.

Obviously, society has asked writers, as a group, to take time out from normal labor to do this special listening and transcribing, and each individual writer has been assigned a certain part of the spectrum. No writer knows—or can know—whether the section that's been assigned to him contains the valuable code that will ultimately benefit the human species or whether his section consists merely of the more common noise or chatter. But obviously, the system can only work if everyone dutifully struggles to do his best with the material that's been given to him, rather than trying to do what has already been assigned to somebody else.

The voice outside my own particular window has repeatedly come back to the subject of sex. And sure, I regret it in a way, or it sometimes upsets me. But if I were to conclude that the voice is fundamentally not to be trusted, where would I be then? The enterprise of writing would have to come to an end for me, because on what basis could I possibly decide to reject what the voice was saying so insistently? The truth is that if I tried to listen to somebody else's voice instead of mine, I wouldn't be able to hear it. And without an outside voice, what would I write down? Who would I listen to? "Me"? It doesn't work that way. So at a certain point—and with a certain sadness, because of how I knew I would be seen by other people—I decided I was going to trust the voice I was hearing. And of course, like every writer, I hope I'll be one of the ones who will be led to do something truly worthwhile. But in another way, it actually doesn't matter whether it's me or not. That's just a game—who did the best? The actually important question is not whether "I" am one of the better cogs in the machine—the important question is whether the whole mechanism of which I'm a part is or is not one of evolution's cleverer species-survival devices, one that might be very helpful—even at the last minute.

Why is sex interesting to write about? To some, that might seem like a rather dumb question. Obviously when someone interested in geology is alone in a room, he or she tends to think a lot about rocks. And I imagine that when many geologists were children, they put pictures having to do with rocks on their bedroom walls. And I would have to guess that geologists find it fun to sit at a desk and write about rocks. So, yes, I find it enjoyable. But apart from that, I still find myself wondering, "Why is it interesting to write about sex?"

One reason is that sex is shocking. Yes, it's still shocking, after all these years—isn't that incredible? At least it's shocking to me. And I suppose I think it's shocking because, even after all these years, most bourgeois people, including me, still walk around with an image of themselves in their heads that doesn't include—well—that. I'm vaguely aware that while going about my daily round of behavior, I'm making use of various mammalian processes, such as breathing, digesting, and getting from place to place by hobbling about on those odd legs we have. But the fact is that when I form a picture of myself, I see myself doing the sorts of things that humans do and only humans do—things like hailing a taxi, going to a restaurant, voting for a candidate in an election, or placing receipts in various piles and adding them up. But if I'm unexpectedly reminded that my soul and body are capable of being totally swept up in a pursuit and an activity that pigs, flies, wolves, lions, and tigers also engage in, my normal picture of myself is violently disrupted. In other words, consciously, I'm aware that I'm a product of evolution, and I'm part of nature. But my unconscious mind is still partially wandering somewhere in the early nineteenth century and doesn't know these things yet.

Writing about sex is really a variant of what Wordsworth did, that is, it's a variant of writing about nature, or as we call it now, "the environment." Sex is "the environment" coming inside, coming into our home or apartment and taking root inside our own minds. It comes out of the mud where the earliest creatures swam; it comes up and appears in our brains in the form of feelings and thoughts. It sometimes appears with such great force that it sweeps other feelings and other thoughts completely out of the way. And on a daily basis it quietly and patiently approaches the self and winds itself around it and through it until no part of the self is unconnected to it.

Sex is of course an extraordinary meeting-place of reality and dream, and it's also—what is not perhaps exactly the same thing— an extraordinary meeting-place of the meaningful and the meaning-less. The big toe, for example, is one part of the human body, human flesh shaped and constructed in a particular way. The penis is an-other part of the body, located not too far away from the big toe and built out of fundamentally the same materials. The act of sex, the particular shapes of the penis and the vagina, are the way they are because natural selection has made them that way. There may be an adaptive value to each particular choice that evolution made, but from our point of view as human beings living our lives, the evolu-tionary explanations are unknown, and the various details present themselves to us as completely arbitrary. It can only be seen as funny that men buy magazines containing pictures of breasts, but not magazines with pictures of knees or forearms. It can only be seen as funny that demagogues give speeches denouncing men who insert their penises into other men's anuses—and then go home to insert their own penises into their wives' vaginas! (One might have thought it obvious that either both of these acts are completely outrageous, or neither of them is.) And yet the interplay and permutations of the apparently meaningless, the desire to penetrate anus or vagina, the glimpse of the naked breast, the hope of sexual intercourse or the failure of it, lead to joy, grief, happiness, or desperation for the human creature.

Perhaps it is the power of sex that has taught us to love the meaningless and thereby turn it into the meaningful. Amazingly, the love of what is arbitrary (which one could alternatively describe as the love of reality) is something we human beings are capable of feeling (and perhaps even what we call the love of the beautiful is simply a particular way of exercising this remarkable ability). So it might not be absurd to say that if you love the body of another person, if you love another person, if you love a meadow, if you love a horse, if you love a painting or a piece of music or the sky at night, then the power of sex is flowing through you.

Yes, some people go through life astounded every day by the beauty of forests and animals; some are astounded more frequently by the beauty of art; and others by the beauty of other human beings. But science could one day discover that the ability to be astounded by the beauty of other human beings came first, and to me it seems implausible to imagine that these different types of astonishment or appreciation are psychologically unrelated.

It's also interesting to write about sex because it's often noted that writers like to write about conflict, and of course conflict is built into the theme of sex. A story about a person who wants to have a plate of spaghetti might be interesting, but a story about a person who wants to have another person—now, that is potentially even more interesting, because the person who is wanted may not want in return. But leaving aside the conflict involved in the fact that people's desires are often at cross purposes, sex has always been known to be such a powerful force that fragile humanity can't help but be terribly nervous in front of it, so powerful barriers have been devised to control it—taboos of all varieties, first of all, and then all the emotions subsumed under the concepts of jealousy and possessiveness, possessiveness being a sort of anticipatory form of jealousy. (I noticed recently that a sociological survey of married people in the United States found that when asked the question: "What is very important for a successful marriage?" the quality mentioned most frequently—by 93 percent of the respondents—was "faithfulness," while "happy sexual relationship" came in with only 70 percent. In other words, to 23 percent of the respondents, it seemed more important that they and their partner should not have sex with others than that they themselves should enjoy sex.)

Sex seems capable of creating anarchy, and those who are committed to predictability and order find themselves inevitably either standing in opposition to it, or occasionally trying to pretend to themselves that it doesn't even exist. My local newspaper, the *New York Times*, for example, does not include images of naked people. Many of its readers might enjoy it much much more if it did, but those same readers still might not buy it if those images were in it, because if it contained such images it couldn't be the *New York Times*, it couldn't present the portrait of a normal, stable, adequate world—a world not ideal, but still good enough—which it's the function of the *New York Times* to present every day. Nudity somehow seems to imply that anything could happen, but the *New York Times* is committed to telling its readers that many things will *not* happen, because the world is under control, benevolent people are looking out for us, the situation is not as bad as we tend to think, and while problems do exist, they can be solved by wise rulers. The contemplation of nudity or sex could tend to bring up the alarming idea that at any moment human passions might rise up and topple the world we know.

But perhaps it would be a good thing if people saw themselves as a part of nature, connected to the environment in which they live. Sex can be a very humbling, equalizing force. It's often been noted that naked people do not wear medals, and weapons are forbidden inside the pleasure garden. When the sexuality of the terrifying people we call "our leaders" is for some reason revealed, they lose some of their power—sometimes all of it—because we're reminded (and strangely, we need reminding) that they are merely creatures like the ordinary worm or beetle that creeps along at the edge of the pond. Sex really is a nation of its own. Those whose allegiance is given to sex at a certain moment withdraw their loyalty temporarily from other powers. It's a symbol of the possibility that we might all defect for one reason or another from the obedient columns in which we march.

A NOTE ON THE TEXT

These pieces appeared previously in different places in slightly different form. As they are now appearing between the covers of a book, and as I'm still alive, I haven't hesitated to fix things that seemed repetitious, illogical, mistaken, garbled, whatever.
—W.S.

SOURCES

1. "The Quest for Superiority" was delivered as the Blashfield Foundation Address on May 21, 2008, at the Ceremonial of the American Academy of Arts and Letters in New York. It was originally published under the title, "The Unobtrusives," reprinted with permission from *Tin House*.

"2. "After the Destruction of the World Trade Center" was originally published as "The Foreign Policy Therapist" in the *Nation*, December 3, 2001.

3. "Morality" was originally published as the Appendix to *Aunt Dan and Lemon*, Grove Weidenfeld, 1985.

4. "An American Publishes a Magazine" was originally published as the Editor's Note in *Final Edition*, Seven Stories Press, 2004.

5. "Patriotism" was originally published in the *Nation*, July 15–22, 1991.

6. Interview with Noam Chomsky originally published in *Final Edition*.

7. "Bush Proposes Preemptive War" was originally published as "The Dangerous Restaurant," in the *Nation*, October 28, 2002.

8. "The Invasion of Iraq Is Moments Away" was originally published as "Fragments from a Diary," in the *Nation*, March 31, 2003.

9. "Up to Our Necks in War" was originally published as "Before the Election—Fragments from a Diary 2004," in *Final Edition*.

10. "Israel Attacks Gaza" was originally published as "Israel in Gaza: Irrationality," on www.thenation.com, December 29, 2008.

11. "Myself and How I Got into the Theatre" was originally published as the Introduction to *Plays One* by Faber & Faber/Faber Contemporary Classics, 1997.

12. "Reading Plays" was originally published as the Author's Note in *Four Plays* by Noonday Press, Farrar, Straus & Giroux, 1997.

13. "Aesthetic Preferences" was originally published as "A Letter to the Reader" in *Our Late Night and A Thought in Three Parts: Two Plays* by Theater Communications Group, 2008.

14. "Interview with Mark Strand" was originally published as "Mark Strand: The Art of Poetry LXXVII" in the *Paris Review*, Fall 1998.

15. "Writing about Sex" was originally published as the Afterword to *Our Late Night and A Thought in Three Parts: Two Plays*.

ABOUT HAYMARKET BOOKS

Haymarket Books is a nonprofit, progressive book distributor and publisher, a project of the Center for Economic Research and Social Change. We believe that activists need to take ideas, history, and politics into the many struggles for social justice today. Learning the lessons of past victories, as well as defeats, can arm a new generation of fighters for a better world. As Karl Marx said, "The philosophers have merely interpreted the world; the point however is to change it."

We take inspiration and courage from our namesakes, the Haymarket Martyrs, who gave their lives fighting for a better world. Their 1886 struggle for the eight-hour day reminds workers around the world that ordinary people can organize and struggle for their own liberation.

For more information and to shop our complete catalog of titles, visit us online at www.haymarketbooks.org.

ALSO FROM HAYMARKET BOOKS

Field Notes on Democracy • Arundhati Roy

Diary of Bergen-Belsen • Hanna Lévy-Hass, foreword by Amira Hass

Hopes and Prospects • Noam Chomsky

In Praise of Barbarians: Essays Against Empire • Mike Davis

Literature and Revolution • Leon Trotsky, Edited by William Keach

Road from ar Ramadi: The Private Rebellion of Staff Sergeant Camilo Mejía: An Iraq War Memoir • Camilo Mejía

Subterranean Fire: A History of Working-Class Radicalism in the United States • Sharon Smith

The Pen and the Sword: Conversations with Edward Said • David Barsamian

The Meaning of Marxism • Paul D'Amato

Sin Patrón: Stories from Argentina's Worker-run Factories • The lavaca collective, preface by Naomi Klein and Avi Lewis